How to Raise All the Money You Need for Any Business

How to Raise All the Money You Need for Any Business

101 QUICK WAYS TO ACQUIRE MONEY FOR ANY BUSINESS PROJECT IN 30 DAYS OR LESS

Tyler G. Hicks

WILEY

John Wiley & Sons, Inc.

Published by John Wiley & Sons, Inc., Hoboken, New Jersey.
Published simultaneously in Canada.

For general information on our other products and services or for technical support,
please contact our Customer Care Department within the United States at (800) 762-
2974, outside the United States at (317) 572-3993 or fax (317) 572-4002.

Wiley also publishes its books in a variety of electronic formats. Some content that
appears in print may not be available in electronic books. For more information about
Wiley products, visit our web site at www.wiley.com.

Library of Congress Cataloging-in-Publication Data:

Hicks, Tyler Gregory
    How to raise all the money you need for any business : 101 quick ways to acquire
money for any business project in 30 days or less / Tyler G. Hicks.
      p. cm.
    Includes index.
    ISBN 978-0-470-19116-3 (pbk.)
      1. Small business—United States—Finance. 2. New business enterprises—
United States—Finance. I. Title.
HG4027.7.H527 2008
658.15'224–dc22

                                                   2008008478

Printed in the United States of America

10 9 8 7 6 5 4 3 2 1

This book is dedicated with thanks to the thousands of borrowers whose loan applications I approved as a loan officer, and whose loan checks I happily signed.

Contents

Preface
WHAT THIS BOOK WILL DO
FOR YOU

In school many of us learned that water is the universal solvent. Yet when we get into the real world of business or income real estate we soon learn that—in most of our lives—*money* is the universal solvent!

So the biggest challenge you, as a beginning or experienced wealth builder, face is raising the money you need to (a) start, (b) buy, or (c) expand your business, or income real estate, activities. This book shows you exactly how and where to raise and get the money you need for your business moneymaking projects of all kinds.

The methods I show you get you started on 100 percent financing—where you don't use any of your own money. These methods are also called *zero-cash financing*. You use other people's money (OPM) to finance your business or real estate deals.

This book gives you hundreds of smart, little-known ways to access the universal solvent needed for every business and real estate endeavor. Using this book, you'll become an expert at using other people's money to build your own wealth in a business or real estate activity of your choice using 100 percent financing.

Even if you have poor credit, a history of bankruptcy, slow pay records, or other financial problems, this book shows you, step-by-step, how to get the business or real estate money you need.

And since most people are in a big hurry today to get the money they need, this book focuses on getting you your money in 30 days, or less. "Patience," I've learned as a loan officer, "falls out of the dictionary when people start looking for financing of any type!" So I help you shorten the time it normally takes to get a loan, a grant, venture capital, or public funding for your business. And remember, when I use the word *business*, I also mean income real estate because it *is* a business!

To be certain you get the money you seek, this book covers (1) loans of every type for business and real estate, (2) venture capital funding, (3) grant money, (4) public funding via stock offerings (public or private), (5) investment trusts, (6) limited partnerships, and so on. Thus, you have a full toolbox of proven methods to raise money for any type of business or real estate you might choose to own today. You become an expert on using OPM to build your wealth.

Since collateralized loans are one of the universal solvents of business ownership, dozens of different types of these loans are covered in this book. Do you need a collateralized loan of some type? Look it up in the chapters on loans and you'll find it discussed there. You'll also learn how to get such a loan for yourself—quickly and easily.

And since owning, and building riches with, your own business usually involves additional funding other than collateralized loans, this book also covers what I call *ink-on-paper* loans—also known as *signature* loans. These loans can provide you with the funding you need for any work that must be done to repair and upgrade machines, prepare leased spaces for your business activities (called *leasehold improvements*), convert empty yards to parking areas, serve as the down payment on income real estate, and so on. You will usually borrow the money you use for such needs. This book shows you how and where to get the money you need for these workplace-related signature loans for business projects. You will also learn how to use the enormous borrowing power of your credit cards to fund any business or income real estate you'd like to own.

To further help you find the business or income real estate financing you need, you are given, in each section covering a specific money type, typical sources of the kind of funding you seek. Along with the how and where of finding the money you need for any business deal, this book also gives you:

- Specific methods for you to use to get 100 percent financing of your business or income real estate via loans, grants, venture capital, private money sources, and public (or private) stock or bond offerings.
- Smart ways for you to apply for the funding you need—be it just a few thousand dollars or multimillions.

- Foolproof 100 percent financing loan, grant, private-money, and venture-capital application methods for you that ensure you'll present completed documents that, by their appearance alone, show that you're organized, businesslike, and reliable.
- Active sources for your business or income real estate money, with focused suggestions on how to prepare winning requests for the money you need.
- Internet methods and sources for getting the business money you need. While the Internet may seem an easy source of funding, you do need know-how to get your best deal. This book gives you that know-how.
- Techniques for getting multiple (more than one) loans for your business and income real estate deals. Multiple loans help you obtain 100 percent financing, or zero-cash financing.
- Methods for making bad or poor credit work for you—that is, act in your favor instead of against you when you apply for a business or real estate loan or grant.
- Ways to get no-repay grant money for a variety of business and income real estate deals. This book even shows you ways to get grants to catch up with delinquent home mortgage payments in some sections of the United States.
- Steps for using co-signers and other proven credit improvement methods to make your credit stronger. This is often called *credit enhancement.*
- Money-borrowing methods for obtaining needed business and income real estate funds from private lenders to speed the loan process while reducing the scrutiny of your money-making activities.
- Proven steps to improve your credit so you're better qualified to get any type of funding you need for your business investments.
- Profitable ways to use the borrowed business money and cash you obtain from grants, venture capital, or public funds.

So come along with me, good friend, and we'll get you started in your career of owning your own business or income real estate using borrowed money, or other people's money. You'll quickly learn how to build riches for yourself in any of more than a hundred businesses of your choice, on borrowed money. And you'll soon see the enormous power of other people's money, and how it can change your life. You'll stop being a wage slave and become the proud and wealthy owner of your own business—using the staggering power of borrowed money and other people's money!

When you subscribe to one of my newsletters (see Appendix) I'll be happy to put you in touch with respected specialty lenders, venture capitalists, grant experts, and other funders who might help you obtain the money you need for a viable business project. I've worked with these people for years and I know them to be ethical, responsible, helpful, and reliable professionals who will never ask you to pay front money or advance fees for their services.

Throughout this book I suggest several important ways for you to get easy, quick funding, in 30 days or less. These ways include using credit card lines of credit, preparing a short business plan, and listening to your lender. The suggestions are based on my years as a loan officer. I repeat these suggestions in various chapters because I know they *do* work. So please use these methods because they make it almost certain that you'll get the business money you need!

On every page, this book focuses on *you*, showing *you* how to get the powerful money *you* need, in 30 days or less. So let's get *you* started getting that universal solvent—borrowed, and other people's, business or real estate money—right now! You'll quickly become a believer in 100 percent financing of business or real estate. And you'll soon be one of my friendly zero-cash enthusiasts!

Tyler G. Hicks

1

Powerful Business Financing Methods for Your Success

Y ou want to start, or buy, a business of your own. And you need money to get started in your own business or income real estate! How can I say this? *Because you're reading this book.* And, as a reader of my book, you're my friend. I'm here to help you get the money you need to start, or buy, a business or real estate property of *your* choice.

When I talk to, or about, ambitious people such as yourself, I refer to them as *beginning wealth builders* (BWBs from now on). In each chapter of this book I'll be your BWB mentor and I'll show you dozens of ways to get the money you need for your chosen business or—in later chapters—income-producing real estate. In some cases I'll even consider being an investor or private lender for your business or real estate.

And if you're an *experienced wealth builder* needing money, I call you an EWB. I'm also here to help you as much as I help BWBs find the money they need, in 30 days or less.

So let's get started getting you the business money you need as quickly as possible—even with not-the-best credit. In showing you how to get the money you seek, I'll introduce you to some unusual methods. Please don't ignore them because they *do* work! They've worked for thousands of people around the world. And— hopefully—they'll work for you, too.

Smart Borrowing Techniques for Any Business

You've heard, I'm sure, the expression, "Knowledge is power." The concept that knowledge is power can easily be applied to getting the money you need for your business. "But how do I get the knowledge to get the power?" you ask.

Your answer is simple. You become a part-time "loan student." Why? Because you can get more loans for yourself if you become a part-time loan student who learns as much as possible about the art of getting business and/or real estate loans. In your part-time study you'll learn to use smart borrowing techniques. These techniques are given throughout this book. And these methods give you powerful, clever, and adroit ways to get loans for yourself. What are some of these techniques? They are:

1. **Apply to lenders** who make your type of loan. Don't go to a real estate lender for a business loan!
2. **Know in advance** that your chosen lender *is* lending. Some lenders stop lending for a few days when they're waiting for the loan demand to change.
3. **Keep your money request in line** with your lender's guidelines. Don't ask for $10 million when the lender's top loan is $5 million.
4. **Type, or prepare on computer,** all loan documents. Doing so increases your chances for approval by 25 percent. How do I know? Because I'm both a public and private lender dealing with business loans every day of the week. I spent years as a loan officer for a large lender, approving millions of dollars in loans to people just like yourself. Typed loan applications always get more attention, sooner, from myself and loan officers at every type of lender!
5. **Don't bug your lender for a fast answer.** Allow the lender time to evaluate your loan application and make a decision.
6. **Accept your lender's terms** for the loan. Don't haggle over a one-quarter point difference in interest rate. And don't try to stretch the term of the loan. Accept the term (number of years for loan payback) and plan on extending the loan after a few years of on-time payment history, if you want to reduce your monthly payments. Any lender will be glad to work with you at that time!

7. **Repay your loan on time**—and in full. If you can make a few advance payments, do so. Then if you're a month late on a payment you won't be penalized. Further, your "late" payment won't go on your record because it is really early for the following month!
8. **Inform your lender** of any address or name changes. When lenders feel that you want to keep them informed about your business, their opinion of you soars. This makes getting your next loan a lot easier!
9. **Be ready to have your lender offer you** a new loan, or extended terms on your current loan, after you've made your 24th payment on a 60-month loan. Accept the offer if it makes financial sense to you. If it doesn't, politely tell your lender you'd like to stay with your current terms because you're so happy with their excellent services. They'll love you!

In my work as a professional and private lender adviser I've seen hundreds of capable BWBs get loans using the techniques listed here that they learned as a part-time loan student. You, too, can do the same. Or you can consult this book and its author, who is a full-time loan student who can help you get the business loan you need, using these techniques.

Find Lenders Having Borrower-Sympathetic Terms

We all know what a sympathetic person is—someone who listens to us and helps us with our problems. So suppose, good friend of mine, that *you* could find a sympathetic lender. This would be a lender whose terms might be sympathetic, such as:

- **Personal loans** and business loans from the same lender.
- **Fast approvals**—often in just one day.
- **No collateral needed** for many of the loans made.
- **Paperwork** of the usual type is not needed.

Wouldn't such a lender delight you? I'm sure it would. Working with such a sympathetic lender to get your business loan would be a pleasure, instead of a pain. You could obtain your business loan sooner, with less paperwork and fewer explanations.

And what's more, such lenders sometimes offer an affiliate program in which you can recommend its services to potential borrowers (including yourself). You'll receive a nice fee when that borrower obtains a loan from the lender.

To be eligible to become an affiliate of such a lender:

- **You must** have an Internet site of a type approved by the lender.
- **You must** run a banner ad supplied by the lender on your Internet site.
- **You must** obey certain simple, and logical, rules the lender sets for you.
- **You must** sign an agreement to abide by the lender's business rules.

These requirements are simple and are normal in any business relationship. Thus, when you agree to borrow from, or represent, another business, that firm:

- **Expects you** to behave in an acceptable business manner.
- **Expects you** to respect its history and its long-established procedures.
- **Expects you** to use its applications and other materials in the way its employees do.
- **Expects you** to treat its employees and customers politely and fairly at all times.

Given these simple requirements and the sympathetic views of such lenders, how should you act toward these lenders to obtain the loan you seek? Here are winning steps to find and get your loan from a sympathetic lender:

1. **Look for lenders** who feature in their print and online ads the sympathetic terms listed earlier. You'll find such lenders in the *International Wealth Success* (IWS) *Newsletter,* described in the Appendix.
2. **Find out which type of loan** your sympathetic lender prefers to make by calling the lender on the phone.
3. **Tailor your loan** to the sympathetic lender's terms.
4. **Give the lender** all the info requested. Don't hold back. The lender wants to make a loan to you.

Deal with a sympathetic lender and expect to get the results you seek.

That's what a sympathetic lender wants to do for you—make the loan you seek!

Become a Loan Expert to Get Your Business Loans

You've heard the saying, "If you can't beat them, join them!" This is what you can do when you're trying to get a business loan for yourself. So how can *you* "join them" to get your loan? You can:

1. **Become** a loan originator for a local lender.
2. **Become** a finder for loans for yourself and clients.
3. **Become** a financial broker for client business loans.

Let's look at each way you might "join them" to get your business loan while becoming a loan expert.

Become a Loan Originator

As a loan originator you can expect to perform the following important and knowledge-building tasks that will blow your mind with business loan data:

- **You find borrowers** (including yourself) in your area for business loans for a local lender, such as a bank.
- **You act as an independent contractor;** you are not on the lender's payroll. All your expenses are paid by yourself.
- **You will earn a commission** on each loan closed for a person (including yourself) that you send to your lender.
- **Your commission can vary.** But the typical payment you'll receive is 40 percent of the lender's loan fee. The lender pays you your commission.

As a loan originator you will get an inside look at how business lending works. You will see which loans are approved, and you'll see which ones are rejected. With your insider's know-how and expertise you will learn how to tailor your business loan for fast approval.

Become a Loan Finder

Work with a variety of lenders—both local and distant. As a finder:

- **Your commission** is paid by your client borrower. Lenders rarely pay finders a commission.
- **You're an independent contractor** working only for yourself and your clients.
- **You can earn much higher commissions** as a finder because the loan deals tend to be larger than those for loan originators.
- **You can work** nationally or internationally as a finder.

As a finder you quickly learn who's lending for what kinds of businesses all over the nation. This valuable information can give you the know-how you need to get the business loan you seek.

Become a Financial Broker

Raise money for companies, help with financing mergers and acquisitions, take a company public. As a financial broker you have a much wider role than as a loan originator or finder. Again, you gain priceless information on who's lending for what kinds of businesses. With a few deft strokes on your loan application you can get the loan you seek.

Become a loan expert and get your business loan sooner, with fewer challenges. Learn what the "ideal business loan is" and make your loan that loan!

Here's a letter from a reader describing his experience as a financial broker:

After reading the materials I ordered from you I decided I was interested in becoming a financial broker. I started part-time and within 90 days I placed my first loan. It was for a real estate deal for just $24,000, but I received 8 percent, or $1,920. This wasn't too bad for the first time.

(*By letter from Virginia*)

Another reader writes:

> I want to thank you for getting me started as a financial broker. I closed my first deal for a $32,000 commission. I was working with another broker in a co-broker arrangement and realized $16,000 with a 50/50 split. Thank you for your personal service and many books. Using ideas from your books, I bought and rehabbed my first property using the HUD 203(k) program. I got one loan that covered the cost of purchase and rehabbing.
>
> *(By letter from North Carolina)*

Get an SBA Guarantee for Your Business Loan

The Small Business Administration (SBA) guarantees loans made to small businesses, such as the one you want to start or buy. Your loan is made by a bank or other SBA-approved lender.

The SBA does not make the loan itself; instead it guarantees a large portion of your loan. Hence, your lender is happy to make your loan. Why? Because if you fail to repay, the SBA repays your lender. It's a win-win for your lender.

Four types of SBA loan guarantees could help you get your business loan faster today. The four guarantees you should look into for your business loan are:

- **The basic 7(a) loan guarantee** that can go as high as $2 million with a fixed or variable interest rate. For your working capital loans, the maximum term (duration) of your loan will be 7 years. Loans for your business equipment, such as machinery, and for your business real estate have a maximum term of 25 years. The interest rate on these loans is tied to the prime rate. The 7(a) loan is great for a business in which you have a factory and machinery.
- **The SBAExpress loan** guarantee covers your business loans up to $350,000 and can be for a revolving line of credit. The

turnaround time for your decision (yes/no) is 36 hours—hence the name *Express*. These loans are made for a variety of business purposes.

- **The SBA Microloan Program** provides guarantees for your business loans up to $35,000, with the average loan being $13,000 at this writing. Loans are made to you by local lenders, with the decision being made by your lender.
- **LowDoc Loan** guarantees are for loans requiring a minimum of paperwork (usually just one sheet on two sides). Such loans are usually smaller than the 7(a) loans and are made for your business start-up or purchase.

You must, of course, qualify for any SBA-guaranteed loan. But most lenders will be more considerate of you when you apply for an SBA-guaranteed loan because the lender has the solid security of the government guarantee on most of the loan.

SBA makes a number of other loan guarantees. These include Export Working Capital Loans, International Trade Loans, Export Express, and many others. You should look into the many loan guarantees available to you by calling the SBA at 1-800-827-5722, or go to the SBA web site at www.sba.gov. You can also contact a local SBA office in your area. See your telephone "Government" pages for its location and telephone number.

My company, IWS, Inc., buys the guaranteed portion of SBA loans as an investment. Why? Because the interest rate is higher than for certificates of deposit (CDs). Further, the government guarantees repayment of the loan!

If you're interested in having us buy the guaranteed portion of your loan (through a brokerage house), you might find it encourages your lender to make the loan to you. Call me to discuss. You'll find full information on how to contact me in the last paragraph of Chapter 8.

Crack the Secret of Good Business Loans for Yourself

There's a little-known source of loans for business and real estate that you should know about. In some cases this source also makes grants for moneymaking business and real estate activities. This source? Your

state, county, or city economic development department. The name
may vary from one region to another, but the function of the group
is the same—to encourage business and income real estate development within the borders of the entity.

Let's take a quick look at some of the types of loans made by
various state and county economic agencies. Not all agencies make
every type of loan you'll find in the following list, but most of them
make many different types of business and income real estate loans
you might need:

- **Small business loans**. These loans can range from $50,000 up
  to $1 million, depending on the agency making the loan and
  how much you need.
- **Minority,** women, veteran, and disabled borrower loans.
- **Energy conservation** (often called *green*) loans and solar
  energy loans.
- **Export-import loans** for various types of active businesses.
- **Pollution-control loans** for air, stream, ground, and environ-
  mental impact loans of various kinds.
- **Seasonal line of credit** for businesses needing quick funds.
- **Short-term lending** for businesses needing quick loans for
  pressing needs.
- **Business and industry** loan programs for machinery, personnel
  training, raw materials, advertising, hiring new help, and so on.
- **SBA loans,** 7(a) general loans, disaster loans, export loans,
  micro loans, and so on.
- **Farm loans** for both beginning and experienced farmers.
- **Real estate loans** for factory, industrial, office, and similar
  buildings.
- **Plus many other types of loans** for businesses in the area
  served by the agency.

So how can you, good friend of mine, get one of these loans?
Contact your state, county, and city economic departments. If you
can't find yours, contact me, as a subscriber to one of my newsletters. We'll find the agencies in your area and give you their name,
address, telephone, fax, and e-mail address in just a day or two.
Remember that your "asset" is being a local business that's entitled
to the type of help previously listed.

To Get Needed Business Money, Go for a Specific Loan

"And what do you mean by a *specific loan?*" you ask. A specific loan is one you get for a named purpose, such as:

- **Purchase of** new machinery for your business.
- **Acquisition of** a truck, airplane, or ship for your business.
- **Improvements for** your factory building or space.
- **Inventory** that you have marketing plans for selling.
- **Purchase of a factory,** warehouse, office building.

Why do we suggest you apply for a *specific* loan? For several important reasons, all of which benefit you:

1. **When you apply for a specific,** defined loan, your lender knows exactly what you want.
2. **Lenders for specific loans** are specialists and they can quickly see if your loan will "fly"—that is, be approved.
3. **Since all lenders want to make loans** (that's their job in life), your loan officer can advise you how your loan application can be improved so it has a greater chance of being accepted.
4. **You increase your loan approval chances** by dealing with a lender that knows your field of business and can offer help to you.

So how can you find lenders for specific loans? You take a number of simple steps, namely:

1. **Write out the type of loan you want to get.** Be specific; use one of the reasons shown earlier, or a variation of it. Thus: You want to buy a new vehicle for your business use. Or: You want to buy inventory to sell. Remember: A lender won't be too interested in talking to you if you don't know the specific type of loan you seek.
2. **Write out the amount of money you need.** Try to name your amount in round numbers. We lenders (yes, I am a private lender and I'm the director of a large lending organization) think in round-number terms. Thus, lenders fully understand

your needing a $100,000 loan. But if you ask for $98,450, as some borrowers do, a lender will be puzzled and his/her thinking will be delayed. Likewise with $846,237 as opposed to a simple $850,000, which any lender can understand in a split second.

3. **Search in any of the sources listed in the Appendix of this book** for lenders making your specific type of loan. Or you can call me as a subscriber to one of our two newsletters, and we'll prepare—free of charge—a list of lenders for *your* loan.

4. **Use the lender's loan application.** Your loan officer is familiar with it and knows where to look for the "goodies"—the reasons for *approving* your loan application. If what he/she wants to see is in your loan application, you have an excellent chance of having your specific-need loan application approved quickly.

Why 100 Percent Financing Is Good for You

When you get 100 percent financing for your business you do not put up any of your own money to buy, start, or expand your business. Thus, you:

1. **Do not draw money out of** your checking or savings account to pay for the business.
2. **Do not sell any assets**—such as stocks, bonds, real estate—to raise money to pay for the business you're buying or starting.
3. **Do not take cash out of** any present holdings to provide the money needed to buy or start your business.

Instead of taking any of these steps, or any others in which you use your own hard-earned money, you:

1. **Borrow the money you need** for the down payment or start-up funds for the business you plan to buy or take over.
2. **Keep your bank accounts** exactly as they are, not removing any money from them to buy the business.
3. **Use OPM—other people's money**—for the down payment and long-term loan for your start-up or purchase costs.

Remember this: With 100 percent financing you usually have two loans: (1) your down payment loan, which is usually 25 percent of your purchase price or start-up cost; and (2) your long-term loan, which is usually 75 percent of the purchase price or start-up cost.

"Does 100 percent financing really work?" you ask. It surely does. And 100 percent financing has worked for years. It's a way for you to get started in your own business when you have little or no start-up or purchase funds. Thus, one reader writes:

> We started our newest venture, a vocational school, using your ideas. We ran one ad in a local medium-size-city newspaper for a 6 percent loan with a 5 percent finder's fee. We got two $100,000 offers within one week.
>
> *(By letter from Ohio)*

The reasons why 100 percent financing is good for you apply to almost everyone:

- **You get started sooner** than if you waited to save up the same amount of money for your down payment or start-up funds.
- **You can often borrow more** than you can save from your salary or other income. Thus, some banks now offer a $100,000 line of credit on their credit cards. Having one of these cards allows you to tap into a relatively large sum of money. With access to funds like this you can get started fast!
- **You work harder at your business** to repay the money you borrowed. Your business then has a better chance of being successful.
- **You improve your credit** as you pay down your loan. Your improved credit means you can borrow more money for your next deal, making future OPM easier to get! Yes, 100 percent financing *does* work! And 100 percent financing can make you rich!

Get Business Loans Using Your Credit Cards

One of the easiest ways to get business loans today is to use your credit card lines of credit. Why is this? Because many credit cards offer very large lines of credit to BWB card holders. There are many advantages to using these lines of credit:

- **Credit cards may offer a minimum of** $5,000 with a maximum of $50,000 on personal credit cards.
- **Business credit cards offer you** lines of credit from $15,000 to $100,000.
- **Your application** for your business credit card is simpler than for a loan for an equivalent amount of money.
- **You can often obtain** several credit cards with high lines of credit, thereby increasing your overall business borrowing power.
- **You never have to say** what you will use the money in your line of credit for, making it easier for you to get the business money you need.
- **The interesting aspect of all this is that** a bank that refuses to make you a business loan of $50,000 may be gladly willing to issue you a business credit card having a $50,000 line of credit!

So how can you get the business, or personal, credit cards you need? The answer is simple, and here it is:

1. **Start with a plan** showing how many credit cards you'll need to give you a total line of credit equal to the amount of loan money you seek.
2. **Find banks or other credit card issuers** in your area that offer business or personal credit cards with suitable lines of credit.
3. **Call, write, or e-mail local card issuers.** Ask for their credit card application. You *must* use the card issuer's application. They will *not* accept another card issuer's application.
4. **Make copies of the application to work on.** Why? Because you want your final application to be beautiful—clean, neatly typed, with a professional appearance that shouts "Approve!"
5. **Talk to your card issuer** on the phone, or in person. Tell him/her that you want to discuss your application *before* any credit checks are made. Why? Because you want to avoid excessive credit checks since they can lower your credit score. Insist on this with your contact person at the bank. Almost all will respect your request and wait until they've seen your application. And that's what you want!

6. **Alter your application** if your contact at the card issuer suggests that you do so. Follow any pointers you're given to improve your application. Doing so will raise your chances for approval enormously. *Remember.* A dollar from a credit card line of credit is the same as a dollar from a loan!

Use Rented or Borrowed Collateral for Business Loans

People like you, with great ideas for a business, may sometimes have less money than ideas. Right? So how can you, or a friend of yours you want to help, get the money needed to start or buy a good business? Here's a way that has worked for many years:

1. **Borrow or rent collateral** that you can pledge for a loan you need, paying a one-time borrowing or rental fee.
2. **Your rental fee** will typically be 5 percent of the amount of the loan the collateral allows you to obtain. Thus, if you get a $100,000 loan using the rented collateral, your one-time fee will be $5,000. This money comes out of your loan.
3. **Any rental fee** is paid *after*, not *before*, you get your loan money. Never pay any money before you get your loan. This is called an advance fee, and you may never see your advance fee again—or the collateral you're seeking. So *never pay an advance fee, also called front money, for any loan!*
4. **You borrow or rent** collateral from someone who owns it. The collateral you use can be actively traded stocks, bonds, certificates of deposit (CDs), bank accounts, real estate, autos, boats, planes, and so on. There is *no* change in ownership of the collateral. There's just a piece of paper showing that the collateral has been pledged to back a business loan. So the owner of the collateral can keep using it. Most borrowed or rented collateral today is in the form of stocks or bonds. Why? They're easy to use at low cost.

Your job, then, is to find someone with an item you can use as collateral for your business loan. How and where do you find someone with suitable collateral to pledge? You can take any of several steps. These steps are:

1. **List your relatives, friends,** business associates who might have suitable collateral to pledge for your loan. Ask each of those having suitable collateral if they'd be willing to allow you to pledge it for a business loan. Offer them the fee I've suggested, 5 percent. If you can negotiate a lower fee—say 4 percent, 3 percent—then do so!

2. **Advertise in local and/or national papers** your need for collateral, offering a fee *after* the loan you need is obtained. Be ready with a business plan for your project. Show this to your prospects. You can advertise free of charge in the *IWS Newsletter* (see Appendix) for rented collateral if you're a subscriber.

3. **Offer an "equity kicker"**—that is, part ownership in the business, or its profits—as all or part of the fee for your use of the collateral.

4. **Get the seller of the business** you're buying to pledge an item you can use as collateral. In turn, you assign part of the business and its income to the seller until you've repaid the loan in full.

5. **Use future income** from sales or rents as your insurance against the collateral you borrow or rent. Then the person you're getting the collateral from will feel safer with you.

6. **Contact a stock broker.** Ask if he/she has wealthy clients seeking a higher return on their stocks or bonds. Present a business plan to the broker to show to interested clients.

Borrowed or rented collateral can be your ticket to future wealth. Today, explore how you can find the rented collateral you need.

Easier Business Financing for You

A new short word is being used today for easier small business financing and start-ups. This word is SOHO—for *small office/home office*. And today you'll see droves of lenders seeking SOHO borrowers to make loans to. For example, a large mortgage lender seeks BWBs needing business financing for a franchise business, or similar start-ups needing funding. The money will be advanced against a home equity loan on the BWB's house, condo, or other real estate, giving the BWB the money he/she needs with as long as 15 years to repay. This means that the monthly payments are much lower than for a typical one-, three-, or five-year business loan from a bank.

What do such offers of financing for start-ups mean to you? They mean several good things for you as a BWB or EWB (experienced wealth builder), namely:

1. **Lenders are now recognizing** that major changes are taking place in the business world.
2. **No longer can lenders look only** for big companies for their loan business.
3. **Instead, there are millions of small businesses** of the SOHO type that need funding.
4. **And these SOHO businesses** have proven to be reliable, well-run organizations that repay their loans on time, and in full, without any collection expenses.

You can take advantage of these new loans today. How? By using proven approaches to raising money for your business in the form of loans. You take these easy steps:

1. **Apply to lenders offering** start-up and franchise business loans to new firms.
2. **Ask each lender** to send the loan application it uses. The lender will send you your loan application free of charge. Some lenders even have a toll-free number you can call so your request is completely free of any charge.
3. **Type the loan application.** Never fill out a business loan application in handwritten form. Why? It shouts "Amateur!" And lenders prefer *not* to lend to amateurs!
4. **Ask for a loan in a manageable amount**—that is, $50,000, $75,000, $100,000, and the like. Round off your required loan amount and your approval time could be cut in half!

Yes, SOHO loans are easier to get today than any other type of business loan. And you can get SOHO money for yourself. Just follow the tips I've outlined.

Use Special Offers to Get Your Business Financing

Lenders often make special offers to get loans out to people needing business financing. (*Remember*: Lenders *want* to make business loans to you because that's the way lenders earn their living!)

Special offers can be your ticket to the financing you need to start, buy, or expand your business. Typical offers may include:

1. **Loan programs for women** who want to start a business of their own. Today, in some areas of the world, more women than men are starting businesses. Lenders with this special offer welcome all women-owned businesses.

2. **Minority loan programs** offered by many banks, cities, and states to members of certain minority groups. If you're a member of such a group and want to start, buy, or expand a business, jump at the chance. Or if you're not a member of such a group but one of your employees is, you may want to form a partnership with that person and borrow the money you both need.

3. **New business loan programs funded,** or guaranteed, by city, state, or federal groups to help you start, buy, or expand your business. Check your local and national governments for such offers.

4. **Native American loan programs** funded by various government groups to members of these communities. Take advantage of all such offers to get the business money you need.

Why can such loan programs, and the many similar ones offered today, be important to you? For several key reasons, namely:

1. **Special-offer loan programs** actively look for borrowers like you who will accept the loans offered. You might as well be one of the recipients of such a loan!

2. **Managers (usually called loan officers)** of special-offer loan programs are anxious to show their bosses how effective and efficient they are. By accepting the business loan money you are helping these loan officers prove themselves as good managers.

3. **By getting in on a special offer early** you'll be one of the first borrowers. You'll get more help and free services from the loan officer you're dealing with. Why? Because at the start of the program, loan officers have more time than later on when they're besieged by applicants.

How can you get in on one or more of these special-offer programs? There are several easy steps for you to take, namely:

1. **Decide what type of special-offer program** you can qualify for—women, minority, Native American, and so forth.
2. **Check locally** with large banks, the SBA, and city and state governments for listings of available programs. Use your local phone book for numbers and addresses. You can also find such programs on the Internet under the agencies you've selected. As a two-year subscriber to our newsletter, *International Wealth Success,* you're entitled to a free listing of such programs in your area. Just ask for it when you subscribe. See the Appendix for details.
3. **Fill out the loan application sent to you** free of charge. Be sure to type the final version you submit to the lender. (As you know, I'm a private lender and I'm director of a large lending organization. Both of us give first attention to neatly typed loan apps!) And, on your loan application, be sure to point out your superior qualifications for getting the loan you seek. We loan officers like to show our bosses how carefully we've selected the applicants to whom we make loans!

There are bundles of business money available to you via special offers. You just have to use your business smarts to find and apply for these special offers.

Go International for Your Business Loans

Do you want to do business worldwide? If you do, there's money available in the form of loans for a variety of work you might do in:

- **Energy**—power generation.
- **Industry**—manufacturing, construction.
- **Agribusiness**—farms, food, crops, and so on.
- **Education**—and training of people.
- **Investment**—financial planning and control.
- **Municipal development**—cities, towns, villages.

Loans for these and other uses are available from the multilateral development banks (MDBs) for various parts of the world. These banks, with their contact data, are:

Asian Development Bank: North American Representative Office, 815 Connecticut Ave. NW, Suite 325, Washington, DC 20006; telephone 1-202-728-1500; fax 1-202-728-1505; www.adb.org/naro/.

African Development Bank: Rue Joseph Anoma, 01 Bp 1387, Abidjan 01, Cote d'Ivoire; telephone 225 20 20 44 44; fax 225 20 20 49 59; e-mail Afdb@afdb.org.

European Bank for Reconstruction and Development (EBRD): One Exchange Square, London EC2A 2JN, United Kingdom; telephone 44 20 7338 6000; fax 44 20 7338 6100; www.ebrd .com.

Inter-American Development Bank: 1300 New York Ave. NW, Washington, DC 20577; telephone 202-623-1000; fax 202-623-3096; e-mail: pic@iadb.org.

The World Bank: 1818 H St. NW, Washington, DC 20433; telephone 202-473-1000; fax 202-477-6391; www.worldbank.org.

"How can I get started getting loans for my international operations?" you ask, good friend of mine. Here are the easy steps for you to take:

1. **Contact the MDB Operations** at the International Trade Administration, U.S. Department of Commerce, 14th St. & Constitution Ave. NW, Room H-11C7, Washington, DC 20230 (telephone 202-482-3399) for more information. You will be welcomed and helped fast.
2. **Ask for help in getting data on loans** you need in various overseas countries where you might be doing business or acting as a consultant for the local government.
3. **You'll receive expert guidance**—free of charge—on what you need to know, and do, to get loans and business at the MDBs. Other data you can get include free information on future opportunities, free financial support, and a guide to helpful electronic media.

Then all you have to do is present information on how your business can help overseas peoples and nations have a better life. Plenty of loans are available for your business if it can help people live a more fulfilling existence.

Use Personal Loans to Fund Your Business

Today thousands of small businesses, and some medium-sized ones, are financed using personal unsecured signature loans. Why is this? Because:

- **Personal signature loans** are widely offered by many different types of lenders all over the country.
- **Speedy approval of personal loans** is a selling feature of some lenders (thus, "the one-hour loan," "the 60-minute loan.")
- **Reduced paperwork** makes personal signature loans easier, and quicker, to obtain by almost every borrower.

To find suitable personal lenders in your area, you can take a few simple steps that are fast and cost almost nothing. So, good friend of mine, take these easy steps starting today if a personal unsecured signature loan will satisfy your money needs:

1. **Figure out how much money you need** for your business. Personal signature loans offered today go up to $50,000 as the top amount. So you should be looking for that amount, or less, per loan.
2. **Locate personal signature loan lenders** in your local area by looking in your telephone Yellow Pages or on the Internet. My firm, IWS, Inc., has a list of 600-plus personal loan lenders available nationwide. You'll find it listed in the Appendix.
3. **Write, call, or fax your selected lenders.** Ask for their lending guidelines and for a loan application. These will be sent to you free of charge.
4. **Make a copy of the loan application** to do trial work on. Why? You want your submitted application to be perfect. You can tweak your entries on the copy of the application so you get it just right.
5. **Be sure your "Use of Funds" reason** agrees with one or more of those listed by the lender. Thus, personal signature loans are made for a variety of purposes, including:
   - Education
   - Vacation
   - Debt consolidation
   - Medical/dental expenses

◆ Taxes
◆ Weddings, engagements
◆ Funerals

6. **Relate your use of funds to your business needs** so that your reason is an accurate statement of what the money is used for. This is extremely important because you do not want to be in a position of giving inaccurate information on your loan application.

7. **Have an exact plan of how and when you will repay** the money you borrow for your personal loan. Remember that every monthly payment you make on your loan helps increase your credit score. As your score rises you will become eligible to borrow more money, should you need it.

Discover the Millions Available from Private Lenders

Many BWBs seek their business money from private lenders. Why do these BWBs search for private lenders? Because their gut tells them that private lenders:

• **Have more flexible lending rules** than most other lenders, such as banks, insurance companies, and so on.
• **Investigate the borrower less** than traditional lenders do because private lenders have fewer checking powers.
• **Make faster decisions** on loans because they do not have a large, slow credit committee or other unwieldy groups that must approve every loan.
• **Often have a greater interest** in the BWB's business success than large impersonal lenders do.

Knowing or sensing all this, a BWB will seek information on hundreds of private lenders. This is a good goal. The only trouble is that:

1. **Private lenders are not easy to find.** Why? Because private lenders often are individuals who seek to invest their own excess money in high-profit-potential ventures. *Note*: It *is* legal for anyone to lend his/her money privately without being licensed as a loan company or a bank.

2. **Private lenders usually make one loan** and then sit back for 6 to 12 months to watch the progress their investment is making in the business.

3. **Private lenders**—as a result—come and go. By that I mean they're in the market to make a loan. But once they make the loan they're out of the market for 6 to 12 months. Then they come back into it again.

Knowing these traits of private lenders, you can improve your chances of getting some of the multimillions available to BWBs every year from private lenders by taking these easy steps:

1. **Start looking for private lenders.** One excellent source is the IWS *Private Money Loan and Funding Kit* listed in the Appendix. It gives you more than 100 active private lenders. Another good source of private lenders is the Sunday business section of large-city newspapers—New York, Los Angeles, Chicago, London, Paris, and so on. Just remember: *Never pay front money (advance fees) to any lender!*
2. **Contact the private lenders you find.** Ask if they finance your type of business. You're much better off dealing with a private lender who knows your type of business and is sympathetic to it. Your loan application is almost half approved when the lender knows your kind of business and likes it.
3. **Follow the suggestions given earlier** in this chapter for typing your loan application and rounding the amount of money you request. Make your application easier to approve and you're almost certain to get approval from your private lender!

Get the Loans You Need Using Specialty Finance

There's a powerful source of money available to you today, my good friend, that's often overlooked by BWBs and even EWBs. The source? It's *specialty finance*. This source:

- **Provides money for specialty or niche businesses**—such as manufacturing, textiles, publishing, environmental ("green") activities, and so on.
- **Provides money in many different forms**—such as loans, venture capital, receivables financing (factoring), leases, and so on.
- **Provides money for just one type of business**—becoming an expert for that type of financing for start-ups, expansions, mergers, and acquisitions.

Why do I suggest that you think of specialty financing for the next source of cash for your business? For several reasons, namely:

1. **Specialty finance firms speak the language** of *your* business and its many facets of money needs and uses.
2. **There's no long period of you explaining** your business to a lender who knows little, or nothing, about it.
3. **This saves you time and energy** in obtaining your loan from a knowledgeable lender.

"What kinds of specialty lenders can I get loans from for my business?" you ask. Here are a number I suggest you check out for your business:

- **Business start-ups**—often called *seed* money.
- **Computers**—personal (laptop, desktop), mainframes, workstations, and so on.
- **Entertainment**—TV, Broadway plays, movies, stage shows, videos, and the like.
- **Estate settlements** and prize winners seeking quick money instead of waiting for final action.
- **Exports**—products and services sold to countries worldwide.
- **Home equity loans** for owners of many types of homes.
- **Home improvement loans** for single- and multifamily properties.
- **Internet projects**—web site design, launching, maintenance, and so forth.
- **Leases**—loans for companies leasing business equipment and vehicles.
- **Mail order** and direct marketing of all types—catalog, Internet, and so on.
- **Manufacturing**—auto aftermarket, aircraft, tools, homes, and so forth.
- **Publishing**—books, newsletters, newspapers, e-books, software, and so on.
- **Real estate**—mortgages of all types, construction, development.
- **Receivables** for businesses of many specialty types.
- **Taxi medallions** for cabs in many cities.
- **Plus many other** types of niche businesses.

Your whole key is getting the right lender for the type of financing your business needs. If you do apply at the right lender you'll find that your chances of approval are much better than when you go to a general lender—such as a bank.

"Where can I find specialty lenders?" you ask. Here are a number of sources:

- **Directories devoted to your business** will often list a number of specialty lenders that focus on your type of business.
- **Newsletters and industry newspapers** devoted to your industry—specialty lenders often run ads in such publications.
- **Internet sites** specializing in news of your business.
- **Financial brokers** who have raised money for others in your type of business.
- **The IWS Newsletter** will prepare lists of specialty lenders for your business if you're a two-year, or longer, subscriber to the newsletter. See the Appendix for details on subscribing.

So if you're in a specialty or niche business, check out the types of lenders listed here. You'll get your money a lot faster, and at a lower interest rate. Take my word for it, good friend of mine.

Jump into Today's New Money Competition

Money is easier to borrow for business today than in the past 25 years. And venture capital (see Chapter 3) is brimming over like never before. In short, money is chasing you—instead of you having to chase money! The reasons for this are:

1. **Banks are competing with each other** to get the money out in loans to businesses and individuals.
2. **Increased bank competition has lowered the interest rate** for almost every kind of business loan you might need.
3. **Intense competition in the field of credit cards** makes more cards available to you to use in your business. Thus, you'll see plenty of business credit cards with lines of credit up to $100,000. Lenders consider a line of credit on a credit card as a loan to you.
4. **Lenders are chasing potential borrowers**, sending them letter after letter asking them to sign up for a business line of credit, business credit card, and so on.

5. **Venture capital firms are looking everywhere** for new, hot, growing companies they can invest in and eventually take public. More on this is in Chapter 3.

With all this courting going on, you might as well get in on it. How can you make some of these business loan dollars yours? Here are easy steps you can take that can bring big money into your business:

1. **Carefully read the "Money Available" ads** in the *IWS Newsletter*, your local large-city Sunday newspaper, and financial newspapers such as the *Wall Street Journal.* You'll probably see one or more banks advertising business loans, lines of credit, and business credit cards. Search the Internet for suitable lenders. You'll find hundreds of Internet lenders in the IWS "Internet Lenders" report.
2. **Contact each lender** by phone, e-mail, fax, or postal mail. Ask for their free information describing their offers for business loans.
3. **Study the material you receive.** Read every part to see how you can qualify for the loans being offered to businesses.
4. **Fill out the loan application** sent to you. Follow the suggestions given earlier in this chapter on typing your loan application, using a copy to refine your information.

There's lots of business money available to you today. All you need to do is start searching for it, using the methods given here.

Obtain Your Business Loans from Local Sources

Many cities and states offer help in getting business loans. But BWBs are often unaware that such help exists in their area because:

- **Loan availability is not well publicized.** Why? Because the agency or group offering loans has a small (or no) budget for advertising.
- **Managers of the loan programs assume** that word will get out to BWBs because their loan offer is so good.

You can overcome this lack of information by taking some simple steps in your area. These steps are:

1. **Look in your city and state telephone lists,** and on the Internet, for a Small Business Development Center (SBDC) in your area or elsewhere in your state.
2. **Call, fax, or write** the SBDC, telling them that you need a business or real estate loan for your business. Ask who you should contact to obtain the loan you need.
3. **Contact the person or organization** whose name you're given. Ask what is needed from you to qualify for the loan you need. You will probably be asked to fill out a short application and supply a concise business plan.
4. **If a business plan is needed**—as is it probably will be—ask for help in its preparation if you have not yet written a plan. Many SBDCs offer free help in writing your business plan. All you need to do is supply information about your business, its competition, and the sales you expect.
5. **Prepare your loan application** using the free help offered by the SBDC. They will even type your loan application because they want to see you get your loan money. Follow the SBDC's advice on what to include in your loan application—these people know what they're doing!

City and state loans offer you a wide choice of financing options. Thus, in one city, the following business finance offers are available:

- **Business start-up loans** for a variety of different types of businesses useful to the community—such as child-care facilities, health clubs, high-tech firms, and so on. Loans can be small (called a *microloan*) to large, ranging from $1,000 to $300,000 or more, depending on the needs of your business.
- **Venture capital for businesses** that promise fast growth in the local area. Fast-growth businesses may include computer and electronics companies with promising futures.
- **Equity funds**—that is, money invested in a company in the form of stock purchases. This money never needs to be repaid to the investors.
- **Grants to businesses** that help the local area with better housing; more medical or health care; programs on the arts, theater, literature, and so on.

All this help is as close to you as your telephone or computer screen. A single, simple call or Internet search can put you on the road to the money you need for your business. Why not make that call or search starting right now. You might raise up to $300,000 with a loan, $500,000 (or more) with venture capital, and up to $100,000 with a grant!

Key Ideas for Successful Business Financing

- **Smart borrowing techniques** can work for any business needing loan money.
- **Find lenders having** borrower-sympathetic terms to get your loan faster.
- **Become a loan expert** to get your business loan.
- **Get an SBA guarantee** for your business loan and you'll have your money faster.
- **Use state, county, or city** development departments for your business loan.
- **Go for the specific,** named loan and you'll get it faster.
- **100 percent financing** is good for you and your business.
- **Using your personal credit cards** can get you the business loan you need.
- **Put the power** of borrowed, or rented, collateral to work to get your loan.
- **SOHO**—small office/home office—loans are easy to get today. Try it!
- **Try special offers** lenders make to get your loan funding.
- **Go international** for your business loans—it works great.
- **Use personal loans** to fund your business.
- **Tap the millions** available for your business from private lenders.
- **Get the loans** you need using specialty finance.
- **New money competition** can put big loans into your business.
- **Use local sources** for your business loans.
- **You have a good friend** in the author, who will help you get the loan you need for your business. You'll find my contact information in the last paragraph in Chapter 8.

CHAPTER

2

Unique Ways to Get Business Money You Need

You *can* get the business money you need if you use unique ways to overcome poor credit, lack of credit history, past credit problems, and other reasons for loan turndowns. This chapter gives you many more unique ways to get the business money you seek.

Five Ways to Raise No-Repay Money

How can you raise money for your business that does not have to be repaid? Here are five ways you can raise no-repay money for your business. Each is a possibility for you—if you have a good business plan for what you want to do.

1. **Get a grant from state, corporate, foundation, or federal sources.** Using the Phone-In/Mail-In technique (see the Appendix for details on the grant kit by that name), you can get a grant sooner and with much less paperwork than in the past. You must, however, perform the tasks for which you're seeking the grant. And these tasks must, in general, benefit a large group of people. Grants are made for a variety of purposes, such as educating the jobless, housing the homeless, restoring a city's historic buildings, improving the health of children and adults, and so on.
2. **Sell stock in your corporation to public or private investors.** By selling less than 50 percent of the authorized shares, you

can retain control of your corporation. An initial public offering (IPO) takes more work than a private offering (PO) in which your shares are handled by a stock brokerage house and resold to its clients in just a few hours. The more promise your business has to grow quickly and profitably, the easier it is to sell shares by either method. Your business *must* be organized as a corporation to sell shares either way. You'll learn more about IPOs in Chapter 5.

3. **Get venture capital for your corporation** by having some of its shares (usually less than 50 percent) bought by a venture capital firm. More control over your firm will be demanded by the venture capital firm than with a public sale of your stock. Why? Because the venture capital firm wants to keep an eye on its money to see that it is well used and protected. See Chapter 3 for more details on raising venture capital today.

4. **Have a foundation make a gift of money to your firm** to fund good work you'll do for a certain group. This money can be given to your firm as a gift payment for work you will do to further the cause for which the foundation was established. You do *not* repay the money—if the work is done. For best results, your firm should be a corporation.

5. **Form a charity to benefit a needy group**—such as the homeless, abandoned children, the terminally ill, AIDS victims, battered women, and so on. In many areas you are allowed to use up to 35 percent of the money you receive for business expenses—rent, salaries, telephone, computer, and similar costs. So if you raise $100,000 you are allowed to spend up to $35,000 on these costs. Just be sure you follow local and national rules when forming your own charity. You should have the advice of an experienced attorney and accountant to guide you in your business activities.

Get Angels to Supply Your Business Money Needs

Today there's an enormous interest in angels of two kinds—heavenly and money angels. This book, my good friend, does not deal in heavenly matters. That's for the men and women of the cloth. Money angels, though, do interest us since:

- **Money angels** provide loan money for new and growing businesses they believe have high growth potential.

- **Money angels** want to be part of your business but seek to stay in the background, out of the limelight.
- **Money angels** are often people who sold a strong business and now want to keep their hand in a similar business without the daily problems and challenges.
- **Money angels** can supply you with quick money—almost overnight in the form of a loan—if they're turned on by your firm.
- **Money angels** can call on their friends to supply extra funds if your angel can't provide all the money you need as a loan.
- **Money angels** usually seek no, or very little, ownership of your firm as payment for the loan help they give you.
- **Money angels** are estimated to total some 250,000 in the United States today, with another 100,000 in the rest of the world. Some estimates say there will be as many as 2 million money angels worldwide in the next 10 years.

How, and where, can you find a suitable angel for your loan money needs? You can take certain proven steps that will hopefully bring an angel into your business life. These steps are:

1. **Prepare a business plan** if you seek loan money for a new business you're just starting.
2. **In your business plan, focus on** the business you intend to start. Thus, your business might be import/export, mail order, financial consulting, income real estate ownership, and so on.
3. **State exactly how much loan money you'll need** for your business. Angels like exact numbers—vagueness will drive them to another similar business that they can get a better handle on.
4. **For a going business,** prepare an ongoing business plan telling where your business will be each year for the next three years.
5. **Contact an angel.** To find one, talk to the people in the association, union, society, or other organization serving your industry. For example, in the plumbing business you have the Plumber's Association, Council, or Union. Such groups often know investors who like your type of business and want to help owners who are starting in it or expanding their activities.
6. **Seek an angel who loves your type of business.** Most angels help the same kind of business they ran themselves before they sold out and started their angel work.

7. **Look for an angel to loan you** anywhere from $5,000 to $500,000 for your new or growing business. Get several of these like-minded lenders together and you can borrow millions.

Yes, there *can* be an angel in your life!—the money kind of angel. And that angel can put you into a heavenly position, money-wise! Try it and see for yourself.

Here's a letter from a reader of mine that shows how powerful your business plan can be:

> After receiving (and using) your great guide on preparing a winning business plan, I have been offered $300,000 to start my innovative bus transportation system.
>
> *(By letter from Washington)*

Use the 125 Percent Loan to Fund Your Business Deals

One of the newest loans around is called the *125 percent loan*. Why is the loan called this? The loan is given this name because of the way it works for owners of collateral who need cash. Your collateral can be machinery, trucks, an industrial building, and so on. Here's an example:

- **Let's say you own** an industrial building worth $500,000 on the market today.
- **You owe** $400,000 on the first mortgage on this building.
- **Your equity** is $500,000 − $400,000 = $100,000.
- **You need money,** we'll say, to pay off other debts, buy a new truck or car, send a child to college, or expand your business.
- **So you apply for** a 125 percent loan. You receive 1.25 × $100,000 = $125,000 in cash from your loan.

"So how does this loan differ from the usual business equity loan?" you ask. The difference is this: With the usual business equity loan,

- **You can borrow** up to 75 percent of your equity in the business equipment or other assets you own.
- **For the business just described,** the usual equity loan would be $0.75 \times \$100,000 = \$75,000$.
- **So your 125 percent loan** gives you $\$125,000 - \$75,000 = \$50,000$ *more cash!* That's a big difference, especially when you're offering the same asset as collateral for the loan.

How can you get such a 125 percent loan? There are several conditions you must meet. If you can't meet the required conditions, you can try to find a business partner who can. Then your partner can put the borrowed cash into your business deal. You'll be the working partner handling daily activities. Your financier will be your silent partner. Conditions that usually must be met are:

1. **The borrower must own** an acceptable business asset of some kind and must have some equity (ownership from paying off some of the debt used to acquire the asset) in the asset. For most loans, you must have owned the asset for at least one year.
2. **The market value** of your asset (i.e., what you could sell it for) must be higher than the amount of money you owe on the asset.
3. **You must find** a 125 percent lender. You'll find such lenders in every large industrial area of the country. Why? Because they want to earn money from this new, attractive loan.
4. **You can find such lenders** by looking in your local large-city Sunday newspaper. Or, if you are a two-year, or longer, subscriber to the *IWS Newsletter* (see Appendix), we will provide you with a list of local lenders free of charge.

So look for a 125 percent loan for yourself. It could give you the money you need for your business—quickly and easily!

Try Unique Loan Sources to Raise Cash

When you're looking for money, you'll soon learn that some businesses are easier to finance than others. Difficult-to-finance businesses can benefit from unique lenders because many traditional lenders shun hard-to-finance deals. Typical hard-to-finance businesses are:

- **Entertainment projects**—movies, TV, DVDs, tape recordings, videos, and the like.

- **Religious places of worship**—churches, synagogues, mosques, and so forth, needing money for expansion or for new construction.
- **Medical and construction receivables financing**—that is, money for health professionals, medical providers, and commercial construction projects, for finished work not yet paid for.
- **Project financing** and loans for small businesses of various types.
- **Nonprofit organization funding,** such as hospitals, colleges, charities, and so on.

To get money for these types of businesses, and similar ones, you can often deal with lenders who specialize in unique money sources. Such lenders are usually staffed by people who were in the business being financed. These people know the business in great detail and they can easily size up a new situation. In dealing with these unique, specialized lenders you'll take these steps:

1. **Get from the lender** their one- or two-page initial information sheet—that is free to you.
2. **Fill out the requested information**—business name, address, telephone, e-mail, Web address, type of business, number of employees, gross sales expected or actually achieved, amount of money needed, intended use of the money, existing loans, pending lawsuits, and so on.
3. **Send your filled-out form** to the lender; you will get an answer in a few days.
4. **Cooperate with the lender.** If you're the one seeking the money, accept the terms (interest rate and loan duration) without fighting. If you're acting for a client, get that person to accept the terms offered by the lender if you feel the terms are fair.

Before you try a specialty lender, I suggest that you, as my good friend, put your project to a reality test, by asking yourself:

1. **Is this a *real* project?** That is, can it really make money for myself and any investors I may get? Will the income be enough for me to repay any loan comfortably, without strain?

2. **Is the amount of money** I'm trying to borrow a sensible amount? This can work two ways for you: (a) The amount you're looking for is too small; (b) the amount you're looking for is too large. Either way, your business could suffer and fail. You don't want that to happen. So get the amount you need right!
3. **Does your business project** have some excitement about it? Will borrowers get involved because your ideas are so different? If so, your funding chances are much greater.

To help you get a group of unique lenders for your business, just ask me, your author and friend, for a list when you become a two-year or longer subscriber to my *Money Watch Bulletin* newsletter, described in the Appendix.

Work with Franchise Lenders to Get Money You Need

Owning a franchised business can be an excellent way for you to get started in your own business. Why do I say this? Because in a franchised business you:

- **Have guidance** from experienced business managers.
- **Have a ready source** of answers to your business questions.
- **Have a business plan** in place, prepared by the franchisor.
- **Have access to** financing from several sources.

Today there are lenders who will lend you money for your future franchise using the equity in your home as collateral for your loan. Such lenders will give you as long as 15 years to repay your loan for your franchise. This means your monthly payments will be much lower than if you were to get a three- or five-year personal loan to pay your franchise start-up fee.

So what does this trend of lending money for franchise start-ups of various kinds mean to you, as a BWB or an EWB? It means several good things, namely:

1. **Lenders are now recognizing** that major changes are taking place in today's business world.
2. **No longer can lenders look** only to big companies for their loan business.

3. **Instead, there are some 10 million** small businesses in the United States that—sooner or later—need loan money.
4. **Most of these small businesses** are well run by responsible owners who repay their loans on time, and in full—without any collection expenses!

You can take advantage of these new loans today. How? By using proven approaches to raising money for your business using small business loans. Just take these easy steps:

1. **Apply to those lenders offering franchise** and start-up loans to new businesses. You'll find such lenders by asking for and studying the loan guidelines they offer in their ads, on Internet sites, and in my newsletter *International Wealth Success,* described in the Appendix.
2. **Ask the lender** to send you their loan application. Fill it out as described in Chapter 1. Some lenders even have toll-free telephone numbers so you can apply over the phone! They fill out your loan application and give you an answer in just a day or so. *Be certain to give an accurate answer to every question you're asked.*
3. **Get complete data on how much money you'll need** *before* you apply for your franchise or start-up loan. You don't want to have to go back for more money when you find you asked for too little. And, as suggested in Chapter 1, round off the amount requested.

Never be afraid to ask for franchise or business start-up money. The funds *are* available. You just have to find out who's making these loans. My company, IWS, Inc., will be glad to help you if you're a subscriber to one of our newsletters.

Use Special Lender Offers to Get Your Loan

Lenders are in the business of making loans. So, just like any other business, they often have what could be called "loan sales" in which they make special offers "to get the money out," as we lenders say. (I'm director of a large lending organization that makes both business and real estate loans.)

At our board of directors meetings we dream up new ways to entice people to borrow money from us. Here are some of the types of loans, and reasons for borrowing, that we and other lenders have come up with, as taken from the ads I've seen:

Emergency loans	No-doc loans	Investor property loans
Expect easy approval	5-day closings	Good, bad, no credit
No application fees	48-hour closings	Bankruptcy okay
Relax—we have the money	Charge-offs okay	Consolidate debts
Direct lender	Stop foreclosure	No application fees
1-hour pre-approval—*free*	125% financing	Lowest rates
Business loans	Mixed-use loans	No closing costs
Self-employed experts	Stated income $	Tough deals okay
No income verification	Bad credit okay	30-minute pre-approval
Credit problems? No problem!	Bridge loans	We'll call you back
No employment required	No-equity loans	Education loans
Vacation loans	Auto/truck loans	Boat loans
Credit line to $150,000	No up-front fees	Easy payments

And there are many more examples I could give you of what we come up with to get the money out! But my space is limited. Note that all the reasons given here are aimed at getting you to borrow some of our money! To get a loan using a lender offer:

1. **Tie your need in with one** or more of the reasons given by the lender. Sometimes an anxious lender who wants to "get the money out" will even suggest an acceptable reason for borrowing. Once, when I needed $15,000 for business, the loan officer at the bank said to me: "The loan committee downtown loves to make loans for office furniture." I suddenly found that I needed new office furniture. And I got the loan for it! So please hear me when I suggest you tie your need to one of your lender's special offers.
2. **Know how much money you need.** No lender will tell you how much money *you* need. You must figure that out for yourself.
3. **Be sure to have** some kind of collateral for your loan. Approval is much faster and much more certain when you can offer collateral for some or all of your loan.

Take advantage of lender offers and you'll be welcomed with open arms. Why? Because "we're all selling something," as a wag once said. Let the lender "sell" you the money you need!

Seven Ways to Get Financing on the Internet Today

The Internet is here to stay. It will be with you for a long time. And you can use the Internet to get financing for your projects by yourself, or with the help of my company, IWS, Inc. To get loans using the Internet:

1. **Decide what type of loan you need.** You must know the type of business loan you need to start your search. Thus, your business loan could be for acquisition (buying) of a business, expansion, machinery, a factory building, and so on.

2. **Find an Internet site listing lenders for business loans.** For fastest results, use the IWS *Directory of 500+ Internet Lenders* that gives you some 500-plus sources of Internet loans of eight different types. The list is described in the Appendix for a price of $50.

3. **Go to the Internet loan site of your choice** and carefully review the offers the lender makes. You must understand the *types of loans* the lender makes, the *typical amounts*, the *interest rate*, the *term*, and any *processing charges*.

4. **Get help if you're not on the Internet yet.** To help you, IWS will do the Internet search for you free of charge if you're a three-year or longer subscriber to the *IWS Newsletter*; see Appendix.

5. **Fill out the loan application online.** Most Internet sites have a form on which you enter the usual data for a loan. The IWS "Internet Loan Sources List" shows a typical online loan application form you can look over so you're familiar with what information is requested. It's good to know in advance what information you'll be asked for.

6. **Click the *Send Now* button** once you've filled out the loan application form on the Internet. Be sure not to click until after you've carefully reviewed your form for the numbers and spelling! One aspect of applying for a loan online is that you seldom talk to a human being. Instead, you "talk" to a computer. Thus, you can't ask a loan officer to hold off checking your credit score until after he/she tells you what your chances are of getting the loan you seek.

7. **Wait to hear from the lender.** Most lenders will reply to you by e-mail to your computer or mobile device. This means you don't have much of a chance of talking with your loan

officer face-to-face to review the loan decision. But you will usually get a fast answer—often in just an hour or so. Internet loan applications do offer speedy results!

Get Mentoring If You're New to Internet Loans

Internet lenders can help you get the money you need for your business. But unless you've had several years experience in borrowing, you should have an adviser or mentor who:

- **Can help you** avoid paying excessive interest rates or fees.
- **Can help you** overcome the fear of investing that most people have. With a hand-holder at your side you feel much safer.
- **Can help** you through the first few hectic days after you acquire, or start, a business project.
- **Can help you** plan your financial future so the money you earn stays with *you*, and doesn't unfairly enrich someone else at your expense.

A good mentor can be a major asset in building your wealth in any business. To find a suitable mentor:

- **Ask family, friends, and business associates** if they know anyone who would like to mentor (advise) you in your search for wealth.
- **Advertise** for mentors in your local weekly newspapers, and in the IWS *Newsletter*. (*IWS Newsletter* subscribers can advertise free of charge.)
- **Carefully interview** people who apply. *Remember:* You're seeking someone with the right knowledge who's sympathetic to your goals. You'll know who's the person for you when the right mentor tells you how he/she can help you!

Tap into New Sources for Your Business Loans

Lenders earn more money from their loans than from any other conservative investment they make. This is why you see so many lenders trying to make loans for new purposes today.

One of the newest loan sources today is **credit unions of many different types** (federally chartered and state chartered) trying to make business loans to increase their income.

- **Today these credit unions** have more than $1 billion in loans to businesses on their books.
- **They want to increase** this amount as quickly as possible by making more business loans.
- **You can get in on this boom** because few people know of the pressures credit unions have to make more profitable loans.

To find out if you can get your business loan from a credit union, take these easy steps:

1. **Get a list of credit unions in your area.** You can probably find them in your telephone book Yellow Pages under "Credit Unions" or on the Internet. IWS can supply a list of credit unions in your state for $25 per state, or free when you're a two-year or longer subscriber to one of our monthly newsletters.

2. **Call (or write) a nearby credit union.** Ask what you must do to become a member. You're usually required to open a savings account in the credit union by depositing $5 to $25. This is *not* a fee; you are free to withdraw the money any time you want to leave the credit union. But you must have an account with the credit union while you have a business loan from it.

3. **Ask what types of business loans are available** from the credit union. If the staff member answering the phone doesn't know whether business loans are made by the credit union, ask to speak to the manager. Business loans are so new with credit unions that not all staff members know about them. But the manager does.

4. **If the credit union makes the type of business loan** you're seeking, join the credit union and apply for your business loan. Joining is free and the credit union staff will be happy to work with you on your business loan.

You'll find that the staff at credit unions are friendly, helpful people. And if your loan makes sense and you have reasonably good credit, you have an excellent chance of being approved. Credit unions have fewer applicants than they'd like to have!

Ten Quick Financing Ideas for Raising Money for Your Business

Today's businesspeople seek quick financing for their deals. You do not want your search for loan money to take months. Here are 10 ways to get quick financing for your business today:

1. **Use a low-doc (minimum paperwork) loan application** for loans up to $50,000. Such loan applications are often just one piece of paper (front and back) that you can fill out in 15 minutes.
2. **Get a no-cost line of credit**—up to $100,000—that's offered by many commercial banks to their business account holders. You'll fill out a short application and you'll get your line of credit. Tap into it any time you need money for your business.
3. **Apply for, and use, business credit card lines of credit.** Card issuers offer lines from $5,000 up to $100,000. Five cards with a line of $100,000 each will give you a total line of $500,000— half a million dollars. Almost any small business can prosper with this size line of credit! Sure, the interest rate may be high, but you can negotiate with your lender to get it reduced.
4. **Get start-up venture capital** from a firm specializing in this type of funding. See Chapter 3 for full details on finding and working with venture capital firms. This no-repay money is easier to manage than a loan.
5. **Find a grant for your business** if the work you do benefits large groups of people. See Chapter 4 for details on getting a variety of grants for your business.
6. **Find private-money lenders** for the money you need. Such lenders are often people who know, and like, your business. They want to invest in such a business without having the day-to-day operating chores that you love to perform. Result? You get the money and the chance to make it grow for yourself and your investor!
7. **Go public with a stock offering** to obtain money that never need be repaid. Chapter 5 shows you exactly how, and where, you can raise large amounts of money for your business.
8. **Use a private stock offering** made by a brokerage house, or yourself, to investors interested in the type of business you

own or propose to start. Again, this money never need be repaid by your business.

9. **Get offshore money from overseas lenders** who are interested in your business and the profits it can earn. It helps if your business has overseas customers or deals with companies or governments in other countries.

10. **Obtain the use of collateral from relatives,** business partners, or others who like the business you're in and want to be part of it. Use this collateral (such as stocks and bonds, real estate, machinery, etc.) to obtain the business loan you need to buy, start, or expand a going business. Your profit from the business will repay the loan you obtain for your business.

Perhaps you have other ideas on how to raise money quickly for your business. If so, great! But one of these 10 ideas may suggest another to you, such as instead of going public by selling stock, do so by selling 25- or 30-year bonds in your corporation. You must eventually repay the bonds, but in 25 or 30 years that will be easy! And the dollars you pay off in 25 to 30 years are worth much less than today's dollars!

Get More Business Loans Using Willing Lenders

Big and small banks and other lenders have discovered small business. "It's about time!" you say. And I agree! In recent months, banks and other lenders have made startling (to them) discoveries, namely that:

- **Small businesses are reliable** loan repayers—that is, they take their debts seriously and *do* repay on time, and in full.
- **Small businesses can be a source** of big profits for lenders— both large and small.
- **Small businesses have assets**, usually have good to excellent credit, and work hard to succeed.

What do these findings mean for you? They mean several good things, namely big and small lenders *welcome* loan applications from small businesses for equipment, buildings, expansion needs, and so on. You can apply to these lenders and be sure of a warm welcome. They want your business! To get a loan from a willing lender:

1. **Ask for the lender's small business loan application**. Some banks will issue a credit card with a line of credit for the amount of the loan you seek. This may be better for you if you don't need all the money at once. Why? Because with a line of credit you don't pay any interest until you use some of the money. With a loan you pay interest from the day the loan is made to you and you receive the funds.

2. **Be sure to apply for the type of loan** the lender is pushing. Why? Because all loan officers like to report to their upper management that their publicity and advertising offering small business loans are producing results—that is, pulling in loan applications.

3. **Ask for the amount the lender is offering.** Many small business lenders are offering loans of $25,000 or less. If you ask for the amount offered, you're right in line with the lender's thinking. And you'll probably get a *yes* answer—quicker than you might think possible!

4. **Send your loan application** to the e-mail, fax, or postal mail address the lender gives you to use. This way your loan application will get into the right hands swiftly. You'll get a faster response, which I hope is *yes*!

5. **Accept any offered loan.** The interest rate won't be too high, so you won't be paying a lofty cost for your loan. Just getting the loan will improve your business and your outlook on life. If you decide you don't need the money, you can always return the funds at almost no cost to yourself and your business.

Yes, getting a small business loan is a lot easier today. Just follow the guidelines outlined here for greater success in getting the money you need.

Ten Ways to Turn Paper into Cash

Turning paper into cash is a good way for you to finance your business or reach important goals, such as:

• **Overcoming poor, or no, credit** without costly charges for credit repair or other types of credit counseling.

- **Acquiring business machinery**, property, or other productive assets to increase your income.
- **Mortgaging out**—that is, getting cash at closing—when you buy a business or assets (machinery, property, etc.).
- **Building a group of businesses**, anywhere from 2 to 100 or more, on little (or no) cash of your own.

"So what," you ask "is the 'paper' you're talking about?" The paper I'm talking about is any document that can be substituted for cash that gives you the same results as putting up cash. Typical paper you might turn into cash includes

1. **A contract you hold** that pays you, or your company, a certain amount of money each year for supplying a product or service.
2. **A lease on real estate property** that gives you a positive cash flow income every year of a stated amount—such as $50,000, $100,000, and so on.
3. **A line of credit** from a credit card company, bank, insurance company, or other financial source.
4. **A gift letter** from a relative stating that the person sending you the letter will give you a stated amount of money that never has to be repaid.
5. **A letter of credit** from a commercial bank, finance company, or other financial institution that can be used as a source of cash for your business.
6. **A promissory note** you have from a borrower stating that you will be repaid a stated amount of money at given intervals (such as monthly) for a certain number of years.
7. **A lawsuit settlement** guaranteeing payment of a certain amount of money over a stated time period.
8. **A purchase money mortgage** you received in place of cash when you sold a business or a piece of property. Paper buyers love giving you cash for such mortgages.
9. **An equity line of credit** for the portion of your business or real estate that you own free and clear.
10. **An approved second mortgage** on your business or property for a stated amount of money that you can tap into when you need it.

Get Loans from "Project-Important" Lenders

There are lenders who say in their ads, "It's the project that's important—not the credit rating." Such lenders usually are:

- **Easier to work with** because they look at the proposed project's potential earnings—not your credit rating.
- **More motivated to make loans** because they have cash they want to put to work earning a good income for themselves.
- **Into the BWB's world** of building wealth with little investment of their own money.
- **Friendlier and easier to talk to,** because most of these lenders are entrepreneurs in their own business.

"So how do I find such lenders?" you ask. Here are your quick guidelines for finding "project-important" lenders. Use these guidelines and you'll find such lenders faster:

1. **Look for lenders who say,** in their business description or ads, "We do the 'hard-to-approve' loans"; "We exploit growth opportunities"; "We are dedicated to connecting investors to fast, easy financing"; "We use our own funds—no loan committee, no lengthy approvals"; or "We provide commercial solutions."
2. **Do a short business plan** (one or two pages) in typed form *before* you contact such a lender. Why? Because your business plan will immediately tell your lender that you're a serious, organized borrower who can be depended on to repay his/ her loan on time, and in full.
3. **Carefully list how much money you need,** for what uses, and for how long. This paints a fast picture for lenders so they can make a quick decision as to whether they're interested in your loan application. You save your time and the lender's time.
4. **Contact your lender** by phone, e-mail, or postal mail. Prepare your request in advance so you know exactly what to say after you introduce yourself, giving your name and the type of business for which you're seeking a loan. Speak clearly and slowly. Don't be nervous! Your lender *wants* to make a loan to you to earn more from his/her cash.
5. **Follow these guidelines;** you'll have a much better chance of getting the loan you need for your business!

I hope you take my suggestions seriously, good friend of mine. Why? Because I'm director of a large lending organization, and we deal daily with loans of many different amounts. Also, I've been a private lender in my own right and made loans to BWBs of many types. So I know, from frontline experience, what a BWB can do to get his/her loan approved.

Try a Working Capital Loan to Keep Cash on Hand

The words *working capital loan* might not sound exciting, but this is one type of loan every BWB and EWB should know about. Working capital loans are key to the success of many businesses. A working capital loan may:

- **Help a new business** pay start-up costs.
- **Help an existing business** cover its expenses.
- **Help a growing business** through its growing pains.
- **Help nearly any business** survive and prosper.

Working capital is cash on hand. A working capital loan is money for everyday operation of the business. And you can use a working capital loan in many ways. For example, you might use such a loan for:

- **Buying equipment** for your business.
- **Paying suppliers** for inventory and materials.
- **Paying employees** and yourself.
- **Paying off** other loans and bills.
- **Helping you** qualify for additional loans.
- **Paying the start-up costs** of your business.
- **Creating a cash fund** for emergencies.
- **Buying or renting** office space.

Every business needs working capital. And every business should have enough working capital to cover the everyday needs listed here. Since this isn't always possible, especially for a new business, a working capital loan can be a real lifesaver. And there are other advantages as well:

- **A working capital loan gives** you actual cash that can help you qualify for additional loans.

- **No collateral is required** by some lenders for working capital loans.
- **Approval of a working capital loan** is not always based on your net worth or financial statements. Still, most lenders want to see a decent credit history and business plan. Having a good relationship with your lender is a big plus.
- **A business with an income** of $10,000 a month might qualify for a working capital loan supplying funds of about $6,000 a month to the business. You pay back the loan each month from your cash flow.
- **Most working capital loans** are short-term lines of credit.
- **Long-term working capital loans** (three- or five-year term) are also available.
- **Exporters use working capital loans** to pay for their shipments.
- **The Small Business Administration (SBA)** and state business agencies can assist you in getting a working capital loan. And be sure to inquire at your local commercial bank about working capital loans available to you.

Use a Loan Application Checklist for Better Loan Results

Checklists can help you get better results when you apply for a business loan. What follows is a 12-step checklist that can help you get the business loan you need—now.

Question	Yes	No
1. Does the lender make the type of loan you seek?		
2. Is the loan amount you seek within the lender's published guidelines?		
3. Are you using the loan application supplied by the lender?		
4. Is your loan application typed throughout, except for the required signature(s)?		
5. Have you supplied data on other sources of income you may have, and the value of any property or other assets you own?		
6. If you're using the money to buy a business, is your debt-ratio coverage 1.5, or higher?		

(Continued)

Question	Yes	No
7. Have you submitted a short business plan with your loan application to show how you will use, and repay, the money you borrow?	_____	_____
8. Have you included, where needed, a title search, appraisal, and insurance coverage data?	_____	_____
9. Have you signed the loan application in the space(s) allowed for your signature(s)?	_____	_____
10. Can you supply a qualified cosigner for the loan if your lender requests one?	_____	_____
11. Have you written a short letter to accompany your loan application so the lender knows where you're coming from when the application arrives?	_____	_____
12. Are you willing to wait until your lender makes a decision on your loan without you calling, writing, e-mailing, or otherwise bugging him/her for a fast answer?	_____	_____

Get Your Business Financed on Zero Cash with a Subject-To Deal

You can get your own business financed on zero cash out of your pocket by using the *subject-to* method. When you use this method to acquire a business, you:

- **Take over** a going profitable business with no (zero) cash down.
- **Assuming any remaining payments** the seller has to make on loans he/she has on the business.
- **You do this without giving the seller** any cash out of your pocket or bank.
- **This gives you an immediate** next-day cash flow from the business.

"But," you ask, "who would allow me to take over a business on zero cash down?" Any number of people, such as:

- **"I've had it up to here"** types who "just want out—fast."
- **Estates that want to unload** a burdensome business that no one in the family knows how to run.

- **Families dealing with divorce or illness** who want to "get away from it all."
- **A seller facing pre-foreclosure of business assets** and trying to protect his/her credit rating and history by getting out before an official foreclosure.

"So what's in it for me?" you ask. Plenty! You take over an income-producing business:

- **With *no* closing costs,** *no* appraisal costs, *no* loan points.
- **With great speed** because there is *no* credit check, *no* bank or mortgage lender approval needed, *no* job check.
- **With great ease;** you can close the deal in the office of the business, or in the living room of the seller.

"But there must be a downside," you say. "Life isn't that perfect." True, there can be a downside, namely:

- **You may have to build** a business up again because some businesses offered this way have been run into the ground.
- **The business equipment** or building may need costly repairs; you may not be able to find new customers quickly.
- **At least three months' expenses** should be in your bank account for the just-in-case situation that may occur.

Buying a business subject to its existing loans means you take over the existing loan payments, after the seller assigns the business to you. It's the ultimate 100 percent financing deal for you!

Always Borrow from Your Greatest Strength

Borrowing money for your business is an art. And once you learn this key art you'll be able to get the financing you need faster than anyone you know. To develop your borrowing skills, take these easy steps:

1. **Borrow from your greatest strength**—(a) your high credit rating, (b) strong collateral you offer, or (c) a qualified cosigner with a strong credit score.

2. **Make your loan application perfect** using the lender's application in a typed format, or an Internet form if your lender requires that approach. Request an easy-to-understand amount—$100,000 instead of $98,763. Be sure to fill in, or explain, empty blanks on the application. Sign and date your loan application.

3. **Apply to lenders** that make the type of loan you need—business, real estate, import-export, and so on. Don't waste your time or the lender's.

4. **Start with local lenders.** They will often give you a faster answer than distant lenders that have to educate themselves about your local values and traditions.

5. **Have a cosigner, guarantor, or co-maker** lined up *before* you submit your loan application. This will save time if the lender asks you for such strengthening, or *credit enhancement*, as it is called.

6. **Present a short (one- or two-page) business plan** with your loan application. Your plan will make a big impression on your loan officer because so few applicants use a plan. And your short business plan may be the key difference between getting and not getting the loan you seek.

7. **Agree to your lender's small demands** for documentation. While it may take a few minutes to find a needed paper or document, if having it means getting the loan, then the time you spend finding the requested paper is well worth it!

8. **Don't quibble with your lender** about the interest rate, term (number of years for the loan payoff), or other features of your loan. All that matters is that you can earn a positive cash flow (PCF) from your business with the proposed terms. Why? Because you will probably be able to refinance in a year or so and get the rate and term you seek. Get your loan while you can. You can refinance later.

9. **Remember that lenders are human—just like yourself.** Treat your lender with respect and consideration. Then the loan personnel will do their best to give you the loan you seek at the rate and term you request—in the fastest time possible.

Use these guidelines and your loan approval is much more certain. Borrow from your greatest strength. Make the loan you need yours! Take my word for it, good friend of mine, because I want *you* to get the loan you need.

Save Your Time with Internet Financing Techniques

You can look for and get financing using Internet sources, as mentioned earlier in this chapter, to speed results. Sometimes your results may be faster than the traditional in-person application. Other times your results may be about the same as with the usual methods of applying in person.

To look for lenders on the Internet you need access to a computer. Not everyone has that access yet. To look for lenders on the Internet you must also know search methods. While these methods are easy to learn, they do take time and effort. But your time and energy investment can bring good results.

To start looking for speedy loans on the Internet you can take these easy steps:

1. **Decide what type of loan you need.** Thus, you'll find that Internet lenders make a variety of loans, such as:
   - Personal loans.
   - Real estate loans.
   - Business loans.
   - No-credit-check loans.
   - Low-doc loans (little paperwork required).
2. **Get the lender's web site or e-mail address** from the concise list shown below. A comprehensive list of 500-plus lenders and venture capitalists is available from IWS.) See the Appendix for the *Directory of 500+ Internet Lenders*. Here's your concise nine-lender-name list:

   Personal loans: www.AmOne.com, www.citifinancial.com, www.loancrew.com

   Private money business loans: www.privatemoneysource.com/hardlenders.php, www.ironwoodcap.com

   Hard money business loans: www.hardmoney-loans.com, www.loan-solution.com

   No-income verification loans: www.fairwaydfw.com, www.seloan.com
3. **Contact your selected lender by e-mail.** Ask the lender to e-mail you info on the types of loans they make; or read it on their web site. Study the information carefully. If you think you can qualify for one or more loans the lender makes, fill out their loan application—usually online.

4. **Take time to enter the data** in your online loan application. Be sure to check your spelling, your numbers, and any reference data you supply. You must avoid any inaccurate statements on your loan application. Follow these hints and you're likely to get the loan you need much sooner on the Internet!

Six Ways to Get Your Business Loan with Less-than-Perfect Credit

Lots of people have less-than-perfect credit. Yet many such people need a loan for their business. So how can a credit-impaired person get a loan today? Here are six practical ways:

1. **Get a cosigner, co-maker, or guarantor** to make your credit stronger. The official name for this is *credit enhancement.* Lenders love a backup for a loan because it means they have a double chance to collect in the event of a problem with the borrower.
2. **Have an anxious seller take out a loan** for the down payment on a business while you work on getting the long-term mortgage. Use the business, and its assets, as collateral for the long-term mortgage. This approach is called a *leveraged buyout.*
3. **Find—by advertising in suitable outlets—an angel** who will invest in your business by pledging suitable assets as collateral for your loan. With solid collateral, the borrower will be welcomed by most lenders, even if the applicant's credit is not the strongest.
4. **Get a partner who has good credit** and have that person apply for the loan that's needed. The person with the weak credit operates the business every day. As payment for his/her loaning of credit to the business, the non-working partner receives an agreed-on portion of the profits. Meanwhile, the one with weak credit works on improving their credit score. Then they can buy the next business without a partner.
5. **Form a corporation or limited liability company** and have that entity apply for the needed loan. This method takes some of the heat off the poor-credit borrower. While the poor-credit borrower may still have to personally guarantee the loan, less attention is usually paid to the guarantor's credit than when they are borrowing for themselves.

6. **Apply at a lender that advertises** by saying "Bad credit? No problem!" or "Bankruptcy OK; Slow Pays OK," or similar statements.

To show you the first of these methods at work, here's an example from my own personal lending activities. As a private lender I lent a licensed chiropractor $25,000 to buy a new X-ray machine for his practice. His credit was a bit shaky, so I asked him to get a cosigner. He did so by asking one of his patients to cosign for him. A lady patient did so and I made the loan. He paid regularly for three months but then stopped paying. We contacted him and he told us that his X-ray machine had been stolen and he could not afford to pay for it. Since we had loaned him the money, we contacted the cosigner. After some negotiation she agreed to repay what was owed us. We did not charge her interest on the amount she repaid. But we did recover the money we lent because we had a cosigner! Many lenders have learned that having a cosigner makes a loan much safer. So get a cosigner if your credit is shaky!

See Your Local Minority- and Women-Owned Banks for Loans

Today minority- and women-owned lenders are booming. There are more than 200 such lenders across the United States. These lenders offer you new opportunities to get loans for your business. Many of these lenders are friendlier and much less demanding in their loan rules. Thus:

- **Minority- and women-owned lenders** usually have strong ties to their communities.
- **Minority lenders are a lifeline** to minority companies in their area and nationwide.
- **Minority- and women-owned banks help** small businesses get started in many different activities—retail, financial, construction, and service businesses.
- **Minority- or women-owned businesses** have a better chance of getting the loan they need from such lenders.
- **Minority-owned lenders have an advantage** over some other lenders because they serve special communities. They pass this advantage on to you, by giving you the loan you need at a competitive interest rate and suitable terms.

- **Minority-owned companies** then pass the advantage along to the local area in the form of jobs, products, and services that benefit the community.
- **Some lenders lend money** exclusively to minority or women-owned businesses. This money can make an enormous difference to these businesses.
- **Some minority lenders provide loans** to both minority-owned businesses in an area, and residents of the entire community.

Minority-owned lenders may be African American, women, Hispanic, Asian, Native American, and so on. As the number of minority lenders increases, they are a whole new source of loans for you. Important minority lenders, according to a recent survey, are:

United Bank of Philadelphia, Philadelphia, PA; telephone 215-351-4600.

Community Commerce Bank, Los Angeles, CA; telephone 323-888-8777.

Ponce de Leon FSB (NY), Bronx, NY; telephone 718-931-9000.

Canyon National Bank, Palm Springs, CA; telephone 760-325-4442.

Peoples Bank, Westville, OK; telephone 918-723-5453.

Key Ideas for Getting Business Loans

- **Use no-repay ways** to get the business money you need.
- **Get angels to supply** your business money needs.
- **Try the 125 percent loan** to fund your business needs.
- **Don't overlook** unique loan sources that can supply your needs.
- **Work with franchise lenders** for your money needs.
- **Use special lender offers** for your business money.
- **Go on the Internet** for your business money sources.
- **Get mentoring** if you're new to Internet loans.
- **Tap into new** sources for your business loans.
- **Use quick financing ideas** to get your business funding.
- **Get more business loans** using willing lenders.
- **Turn paper into cash** to raise the money you need.

- **Look for "project-important" lenders** to supply your money.
- **Use a working capital loan** to keep cash on hand.
- **Check your loan application carefully** before you submit it.
- **Try the subject-to way** to get your business loan.
- **Save time when applying** by using Internet loan sources.
- **Get your business loan,** even with poor credit.
- **Use minority- and women-owned banks** for your business loans.
- **You have a good friend** in the author. You'll find my contact information in the last paragraph of Chapter 8.

3

Successful Venture Capital Funding for Your Business

Venture capital has many advantages for you and your business. These advantages include:

- **No monthly principal and interest** (P&I) payments like you have with a loan are needed when you have venture capital funding.
- **No interest charges**—the money you get is an investment, not a loan. An investment is the purchase of stock in your corporation.
- **No loan applications to fill out**—you will usually get your money on the strength of your business plan.
- **No credit check**—you get your money based on the quality of your business, not your credit score.

Requirements You Must Meet to Get Venture Capital

You and your business must meet certain requirements to be eligible for venture capital. These requirements are:

- **Your business** must be organized as, and chartered as, a corporation.
- **Your business** must be authorized by its corporate charter to issue stock; this is known as the sale of equity in your corporation.

- **Your business** corporation must have a board of directors, as required by its charter. Your board need not be paid anything for serving your corporation. You can have a one-person board—yourself, if you wish. But most corporations have several persons on their board.
- **Your business** must have an Employer Identification Number (EIN) issued by the Internal Revenue Service (IRS) at no cost to you. Today you can apply for and obtain your corporate EIN on the Internet at the www.irs.gov web site.
- **Your business** must have a legitimate reason for its existence— that is, the activity in which the business will strive to earn money must have a reasonable chance for success.

While these requirements may seem difficult, they really are not. Most of these requirements are covered by your corporate charter, so you don't have to do anything special to comply with them.

What Venture Capital Can Do for Your Business

Venture capital is a direct cash infusion into your business. Thus, venture capital:

1. **Gives you** *seed* **cash** for the early development of your business idea, allowing you to construct a product, research a service, and explore market possibilities for your business.
2. **Gives you additional** *start-up* **money** if your business idea proves promising. You use this money to hire needed personnel (managers, production workers, salespeople, and so on).
3. **Gives you** *first-stage* **financing** to grow your company into a healthy, viable business that will expand rapidly.
4. **Gives you additional needed financing** (*second-stage* and *mezzanine*) for the later stages of your business growth and expansion.

Hence, venture capital offers you many advantages for your new or growing business. This chapter shows you how to acquire the venture capital you need for your business.

Businesses having the best chance of getting seed capital at the time of this writing are:

- **Internet firms** offering new ways to serve the public and companies faster, and in a lower-cost manner.
- **Computer hardware and software companies** having ways and products that improve computer usage in small and large firms worldwide.
- **Medical-treatment facilities,** nursing homes, and long-term care centers catering to large groups of people.
- **Disease handling and treatment methods** for fatal and crippling conditions that affect large groups of people—diabetes, cancer, heart disease, AIDS, and so on.
- **Child care,** health care, education, and protection in all levels of society everywhere in the world.
- **Identity-theft protection** for people of all ages who use credit cards, debit cards, and other forms of publicly accessed credit.
- **Anti-terrorism activities and equipment** in many different fields—transportation (aircraft, ships, trains, trucks), public events (sports events, conventions, etc.), housing, educational facilities, government buildings, the military, and so on.

Develop a business idea for any of these topics and you are almost certain to be able to raise seed capital. The world hungers for solutions and you can earn big money providing just one good answer to one of these problems.

To show you how many opportunities you have for seed venture capital today, here are the types of investments a highly respected seed venture capital firm states that it will consider:

- Aerospace.
- Agriculture.
- Biotech.
- Broadcasting (radio, TV).
- Communications (wire, wireless).
- Computer hardware (from laptops to mega computers).
- Computer software (consumer and commercial).
- Distribution (land, sea, air).
- E-commerce (Internet sales and marketing).
- Electronics (consumer, commercial).
- Energy (conservation, green technology).
- Entertainment (movies, TV, theater, Internet).

- Environmental engineering.
- Financial services (banking, brokerage houses, investments).
- Fishing industries.
- Forestry (lumbering, natural resources).
- Genetic engineering.
- Health care (hospitals, nursing homes, hospices).
- High tech (computers, electronics, space exploration).
- Industrial manufacturing and products.
- Information technology (computers, Internet, wireless phones).
- Internet applications and marketing.
- Life sciences (biology, genetic engineering).
- Manufacturing (industrial products of many types).
- Medical equipment (X-ray, scanning, diagnostic).
- Medical supplies (bandages, thermometers, treatment medicines).
- Mining (fuels, metals).
- Publishing (books, newspapers, newsletters).
- Services for businesses and consumers.

With such a large number of business activities being considered by this seed venture firm, you have a major chance to get funded. And this is just one of many hundreds of venture capital firms avidly seeking good deals to invest in today!

Look for Venture Capitalists for Your Special Business

Most venture capitalists are specialists. That is, the usual venture capital firm:

1. **Seeks to invest in businesses** it feels comfortable with—such as computers, medical equipment, electronics, software, bio-fuels, green technology, and so on.
2. **Has people on staff** who understand the particular businesses the firm favors for investments.
3. **Gives faster funding** to businesses it knows than to unfamiliar businesses.
4. **Requires less paperwork** and explanations for familiar businesses.

What does this mean to you and your special business? It means a lot, namely:

- **Apply to the right venture capitalist**—that is, one who specializes in your kind of business—and you'll save time and money. You'll also get faster answers to your requests!
- **Emphasize to the venture capitalist** that your business is of the type he/she knows a lot about and prefers to fund, based on information you have about his/her firm. You'll find an open office door and a welcome handshake!
- **Compare, in your letter or e-mail** to the venture capitalist, your special business to other similar businesses that have done well in the market. Your examples need not be exact duplicates (there probably aren't any), just similar businesses.

Get Your Venture Capital the Easy Way

Most corporations looking for venture capital are new businesses. Few have any sales history. Why? Because the founder usually has a good idea or product and thinks it will earn buckets of money. But the founder can't get started because he/she is short of cash. What can you do if you're in this situation? You can:

1. **Contact** *seed capital* venture capital firms locally or nationally.
2. **Ask for seed money** to take your idea or product into the prototype phase for market testing.
3. **Request a promise of more money** in the future if the business idea or product catches on with strong sales.
4. **Get the start-up money** or build-out money to expand your business and hire management people as sales rise. The start-up money is in addition to your seed capital.

There are a number of seed venture capital firms in business today. Several are listed at the end of this chapter to help you get started. Your approach to any seed capital firm is the same, no matter how little ($500,000, or less) or how much ($5 million or more) seed venture capital you need. You:

1. **Prepare** a 300- to 500-word executive summary of your business, as shown in the following sample.

2. **Send** your executive summary to a seed capital venture capitalist with a short letter describing your company and its request.
3. **Wait** to hear from the seed capital venture capitalist. Reputable firms will usually give you a quick answer.

To show how easy it is to write your executive summary, here's the summary for a computer research and sales business:

Executive Summary for Strategic Computer Corporation

The Strategic Computer Corporation (the Company) is a start-up computer business founded this year, 2 _____. The major business activity of the Company will be advanced research to develop new, user-friendly laptop and desktop computers. Skilled and experienced scientists will be used on an outsourced basis to develop new ways to design and build computers for both corporate and consumer clients. Further, a computer training division will offer educational courses to both buyers of computers and employees of corporate customers. This division will also train scientists and engineers in the methods of advanced design of all types of computers. As an arm of its research results, the Company will sell, service, and repair the laptop and desktop computers it designs and builds for both corporate and consumer clients. The Company will be staffed by experienced computer scientists; software engineers; computer salespeople; service, repair and educational personnel, drawn from many different sources—research laboratories, computer manufacturers, retail establishments, and educational institutions.

By offering a full computer experience to customers—research, manufacturing, sales, service, repair, and education—the Company expects to outsell competitors who offer only sales, or only repair, or only training. Thus, the Company will be a one-stop source for the advanced computer needs of individuals and companies of all sizes—from the smallest to the largest.

To start, staff, and house the Company, venture capital of $25 million is needed. Sales projections show that within three years the Company's revenue will be triple the amount of the initial venture capital investment. The experienced research and management team assembled for the Company knows that their full-service offer will far outsell all competitors. A full business plan for Strategic Computer Company is available from the Company president, Anthony Green, at 123 Main St, Red River, AR 45678; telephone 267-123-4567.

The business in the executive summary you just read is usually called *high-tech* by venture capitalists because it involves advanced technology research—in this case, in the computer and electronics fields. Some venture capital firms prefer high-tech deals because they believe they can make more money financing such companies.

Low-tech companies are those that venture capitalists see as serving more ordinary business needs—such as retailing, home building, and service businesses of many types. Here's an executive summary for a low-tech company seeking venture capital:

Executive Summary for Entertainment Services Corporation

Entertainment Services Corporation (the Company) will provide a DVD, CD, and videotape rental system and inventory of entertainment and educational products targeted at the convenience store market. A number of convenience store chains have expressed strong interest in immediate installation of such systems in multiple outlets to serve their growing customer base and its demand for low-cost home rental of entertainment and educational DVDs, CDs, and videotapes.

The Company's "Convenience Video" (CV) unit is simple and trouble-free. It dispenses, on demand, DVDs, CDs, or videotapes requested by the customer. A nominal daily rental fee is charged to the customer. To provide this service, all the store operator need do is plug the CV unit into the nearest electrical outlet and it is up and running. Key features of the CV unit are proprietary and patented. Likewise, the software to operate the CV unit is copyrighted. Central to the Company's CV unit is the CV data center. This center tracks the selections and usage history of each CV unit.

An experienced management team is in place. Seasoned personnel with marketing, manufacturing, retailing, and management experience are on board.

Sales and marketing objectives promise significant profits for investors in the Company. An initial input of $10 million in venture capital is needed as seed money for the Company. Financial projections show that the Company can produce sales of this amount in its first two years.

The many advantages offered by the CV system make it an important potential leader in the national and international convenience store consumer entertainment and educational field. Investors have the possibility of strong growth beyond that normally experienced in consumer projects.

Full information on this interesting and profitable opportunity is available from the Company at _____, Attn. _____, President.

Here's an example of the letter you can use to submit your executive summary to your selected seed venture capitalist. Alter the letter as you wish to suit your particular needs.

Letter to Accompany Your Executive Summary

Your Company Letterhead
Address
Telephone/Fax Numbers

Date

XY Venture Capital
Address

Dear _____:
Enclosed is the Executive Summary for our Company that is in the type of business you have previously funded with venture capital.

As this Executive Summary shows, our Company has a strong promise of rapid growth in its field. If this Executive Summary interests you, a full Business Plan can be provided.

Very truly yours,

(Your name and title)

Getting from Your Executive Summary to the Cash

Up to this point we've suggested that you use your executive summary to interest a venture capitalist in your project. To get from your executive summary to the seed cash you seek, you'll need a full business plan covering your proposed (or existing) business. While I know that writing a full business plan may frighten some BWBs, yourself included, you will find that preparing your business plan:

- **Gives you a view** of your business that you've never had before.
- **Helps you analyze** your personal and business goals in great depth.
- **Shows you who** your real competitors are and what strengths they have in the marketplace.

- **Guides you into the best way** to run your business for the largest profits for yourself.

Sure, I know that writing your business plan is a chore. But once you do it you will be rewarded far beyond the time and energy you spend writing your plan. And you'll thank me for urging you to do it—as hundreds of BWBs have. I remember a few BWBs who cursed at me when I insisted that they needed a business plan to get their seed capital. But they returned sometime later to apologize and thank me—after they got their seed money!

To write your business plan, start with an outline. Here's the outline suggested by many venture capitalists I do business with. Using this outline will ensure that your business plan has an accepted form familiar to venture capitalists everywhere.

Business Plan Outline

1. **The Executive Summary.** See the examples given earlier in this chapter.
2. **The Business.** Describe what your business is, why you want to go into it (or are in it), and the advantages of your approach to the business over that of any other competing firms in the same business. Define your business model and why it will succeed and prosper.
3. **Financial and Position Goals.** State what profits you seek for the company in three years, in five years, and where the company will be positioned in the industry and with respect to the competition in the same periods.
4. **Products or Services Offered.** Describe what they are and why they will outsell the competition. List the advantages your product offers to its buyers and users.
5. **Your Market.** State how many people, companies, or other buying or using units exist, where they are, and what they're willing to pay for what you'll offer them.
6. **Competition.** Who are they, what do they sell, which advantages do they have, what are their drawbacks (negatives), and how do you plan to outsell the competition?
7. **Use of Proceeds.** Describe how your company will use the money the venture capitalist provides. Give complete details on the use of funds for machinery, advertising, personnel, staff training, marketing, real estate (if needed), and promotion.

8. **Marketing Strategies.** Name steps that will maximize the money invested in both the company and its marketing programs.

9. **Promotion Strategies.** Describe strategies that will publicize the company, its products, services, personnel, guarantees, and helpful customer relations.

10. **Description of the Offer.** What will the venture capitalists receive when they invest their money in your corporation? Be specific—state the number of shares they will receive and the par value of each. (*Par value* is the monetary value assigned to stock in a corporation when a company is started. This value might be 1 cent per share, 10 cents per share, $1 per share. Most stock is valued, and sold, at a price much higher than the par value.)

11. **Pro Forma Financial Statements.** *Pro forma* means "provided in advance" and refers to financial statements (profit and loss) that you construct based on the income and expenses you expect your company to have in future years. You provide your estimates for the first three years of the business. Give the month-to-month estimates on the firm's income, expenses, and profits so your venture capitalist can easily see trends in your sales and profits.

12. **Warnings to Investors.** If your company is a new one, be sure to point out the risks investors face. Tell what may (or could) go wrong. Don't be afraid of scaring venture capitalists! They've seen all this before and know what risks every new business faces. Tell it as it is and your chances of getting the big bucks are much, much greater than if you try to deny what everyone knows: Business is risk-taking. Your warnings to investors can be run at both the beginning and end of your business plan.

While we'd like to show you a full business plan here, there isn't enough space in this book to do so. However, the *Business Plan Kit*, described in the Appendix, gives you several actual business plans you can follow in preparing your own plan.

Once you have your business plan finished, send it to the venture capitalist that showed interest in your executive summary. Here's a letter you can use to send your business plan. Change it as you wish to fit your deal:

Letter to Accompany Your Business Plan

Your Company Letterhead
Address
Telephone/Fax Numbers

Date

XY Venture Capital
Address

Dear _____:
As you will recall, you expressed interest in our Executive Summary and requested that we submit a full Business Plan.

Our full Business Plan is enclosed. If you have any questions about it you can reach me at the numbers above.

We look forward to a positive response from you.

Very truly yours,

(Your name and title)

Sure Turndowns You Must Avoid

Venture capitalists look for certain positive features in the companies they fund. Here are some of the turndown reasons you must avoid if you want to get fast venture capital funding with additional money (called *rounds*) as your business grows:

- **Amounts less than $100,000.** It costs just as much to process a $100,000 deal as a $1 million deal! *Remember this:* Additional funding rarely hurts a business. You can always put the extra funds to work in safe, government-guaranteed savings accounts until you need the money. So ask for a little more than your numbers tell you is needed.
- **One-person companies.** Venture capitalists like depth of management. You should have at least two people at the start with others to call on as your company grows.
- **Slow-growth businesses** having little future potential. Coin laundries, dry-cleaning stores, and nonfranchised restaurants are such businesses.

- **Unique special-skills businesses** (such as artists, sculptors, poets, writers) where the product output depends on just one person's skills.
- **Fundings that are usually done with loans**, such as long-term real estate mortgages. Such financing is a loan, not venture capital.

Venture capitalists seek to put their money into businesses that have these characteristics:

- Fast growth.
- Competitive advantages in the marketplace.
- Unique products or services.
- Strong management.
- Owners with a powerful drive for success.
- The right numbers for investment and growth.

You can get the venture capital you seek. To do so, you must have the right deal, well presented. Use the tips in this chapter and your chances of getting the venture capital you need will be much greater.

And while you're looking for your seed capital, keep in mind that certain sections of the United States are more likely to receive venture capital funding than others. Here are the most popular areas for venture capital, as reported in a recent survey by a large accounting firm:

1. Northern California
2. New England
3. New York metro area
4. Southeast
5. Midwest
6. Texas
7. Los Angeles/Orange County
8. San Diego
9. Philadelphia
10. Washington, D.C., metro area

What to Do If Your Business Plan Is Turned Down

Suppose that, after expressing interest in your business plan, the venture capitalist rejects it. What should you do next? The first steps are:

- **Don't give up! Keep looking.** A venture capitalist may reject your business plan for any number of reasons not related to you or your plan.
- **Consider using a finder** to locate a venture capitalist that will fund your business plan.
- **Prepare a finder's fee agreement** such as the one shown below, to cover the amount you will pay a finder if he/she finds the venture capital you seek. A number of seed capital deals are funded using the services of a finder.
- *Never* **pay front money** or an advance fee to a Finder! You pay *only* after your company has received the money the Finder agreed to locate for you!

Finder Agreement

_____ hereafter called the Finder, and
_____, hereafter termed the Client, hereby declare and agree, on this _____ day of _____, that the Finder will be paid a fee of $ _____ to find for the Client the following: _____.

This fee will paid to the Finder by the Client within 10 (ten) days after the Finder has delivered to the Client, or arranged for delivery to the Client, the above-mentioned funding.

This Agreement may be assigned to a third party, but the entire Agreement must be assigned—that is, it cannot be assigned in parts.

As evidence of their consent to this Agreement, both the Client and Finder have signed this Agreement as shown below.

Client Name & Title _____
Date _____
Witness _____
Date _____
Finder Name & Title _____
Date _____
Witness _____
Date _____

"What can I do if a finder can't get the venture capital I need?" you ask. Your next step is to try venture capital clubs. Here's how you can find money with such clubs.

Get Your Business Money through a Venture Capital Club

Venture capital clubs are organizations of investors seeking promising new (and existing) firms into which they can put their money with the hope of rapid growth for it. Most venture capital clubs are comprised of local investor members (often called *Angels*) seeking companies in their area in which they can invest. Some clubs also invest nationally and internationally.

To obtain funding through a venture capital club you attend a monthly meeting, often a breakfast. The usual meeting is divided into three parts:

1. **A one hour get-to-know-you gathering** over coffee and breakfast (or lunch or dinner) at which you meet venture capitalists and other investors seeking companies in which they can take a financial interest.
2. **A talk by a venture capitalist** or investor describing the kinds of investments being sought. This talk can be most helpful to you because it lets you see the kinds of deals venture capitalists and investors are seeking. The talk might even convince you to highlight a few features of your company that you hadn't thought of before.
3. **You make a two-minute or longer presentation** about your business, its features, and its growth potential to the audience. Today many BWBs use visuals to give details about their company and business. You'll find PowerPoint, DVD, and CD presentations at many venture capital clubs. Any venture capitalists present can ask you questions about your business. Typical questions you must be ready to answer concisely include:
   - **What makes** your company different from its competitors?
   - **Why do you think** your product (or service) will outsell those already available?
   - **Has your research** or market survey revealed any new areas into which you can sell your product or service?
   - **What are your financial projections** for your first three years of your business operations?
   - **Who's on your management team** and what have they accomplished before they became associated with your company?

- **What are your plans** for future rounds of financing after you obtain your seed capital?
- **Have you made presentations** for this company to any other venture capital clubs? If so, which one(s)? What was the outcome of your presentation(s)?

If you give suitable answers to these questions there's a good chance you'll get the seed venture capital you need. If your answers don't ring a bell, just try again at the next meeting. Why? Because different venture capitalists will probably be in attendance. You may score with them, if your deal is really promising!

To help you find a suitable venture capital club, several sources of such clubs are listed at the end of this chapter. While making a presentation to a club may seem like a chore, your rewards can be enormous. Just imagine getting an infusion of millions of dollars into your company on the basis of your presentation to a venture capital club, plus submission of your full business plan to a club!

For smaller amounts of venture capital—$25,000 to $500,000—you'll find that angel networks may be your best source of funding. Angel networks are comprised of individuals seeking to put excess money to work in a business they think will grow quickly and reward them a better than average return on their money.

Angel networks are often part of venture capital clubs. But there are separate angel networks that function like clubs but prefer to call themselves angels, angel networks, band of angels, alliance of angels, angel investors, and so on. You'll find many such groups in the *IWS Newsletter* listed in the Appendix. And there's a comprehensive nationwide listing in the *Venture Capital Funding Kit*, also listed in the Appendix.

If a venture capital club or group of angels do not work in raising your seed capital, you can always try a venture capital incubator.

Seek Incubator Help for Your Seed Capital

An incubator is an organization that helps start-up firms by providing office space at little cost, plus secretarial, telephone, fax, and Internet services. Incubators may be located on a university campus, in low-cost factory or industrial buildings, or in an office mall or park. Most incubators also offer business advice to start-up firms, along with sources of venture capital.

"Why should I go into a business incubator?" you ask. For a number of good reasons, namely:

- **You work** in a business environment alongside other start-up entrepreneurs.
- **You work** in the midst of moneyed investors who want to put their funds into promising start-ups.
- **You work** with experienced businesspeople who may offer mentoring advice when you need it.
- **You work** in an area that might be financed by venture capital companies. Some of these companies might even operate your firm during its start-up and product-proving phases.

To get started in an incubator, check with local universities or colleges to see if such facilities are available in your area. If not, contact the National Business Incubation Association, 20 E. Circle Dr., #37198, Athens, OH 45701-3571; telephone 740-593-4331; fax 740-593-1996. This Association can give you details about any incubators near you.

Hundreds of successful companies have grown from incubators to strong places in their field. You, too, can grow your company with the help of an incubator and venture capital. Get started today!

Get Additional Funding As Your Business Grows

The beauty of venture capital is that you can get additional money for your company as its business grows. The usual stages of venture capital are:

- **Seed venture capital**, which we've been helping you get in this chapter, is used to show that your product or service can compete in its market and earn money for the investors in your company.
- **Start-up venture capital** is advanced to you after the seed venture capital you received proves that your product or service idea can and will make money for investors. You use your start-up venture capital to hire needed people—production workers, salespeople, managers, accountants, and so on, and get production going.
- **First-stage venture capital** follows your start-up money so you can expand production, advertising, marketing, publicity,

and other functions to expand your business. When you get first-stage venture capital you have a real business that can make you a millionaire sooner than you might imagine!

- **Second-stage venture capital** follows your first-stage venture capital, allowing you to expand your company quickly. For example, the demand for and cost of providing your products or services may exceed the amount of cash coming into your business. Second-stage venture capital will provide the money you need to deliver the products or services your customers are demanding. Again, a second-stage venture capital infusion is an excellent sign that your business is healthy and growing rapidly.

- **Mezzanine venture capital** can follow second-stage venture capital when you need more money for machinery, buildings, personnel, and so forth, because your business is rapidly expanding. You know you need mezzanine financing when your products or services are "flying out the door" or "flying off the shelves," as people say about rapidly selling items or services. Again, when you reach the mezzanine level of venture capital financing, you're in a very strong position.

- **Go-public venture capital,** also called *bridge venture capital,* gets your company to the point every venture capitalist dreams of—going public. When you go public some of the shares in your corporation are sold to the investing public. This is where the venture capitalist earns his/her money. For example, if the venture capitalist paid $10 per share when initially investing in your corporation and the same shares are offered to the public at $50 each, the venture capitalist earns $50 − $10 = $40 per share. Such earnings far exceed what the same money might have earned in an interest-bearing savings account. That's why venture capitalists love to invest in growing companies. Your corporation's growth helps make the venture capitalist rich! And that's the name of the game. And—of course—your corporation's growth can make you rich, too!

Finding Later-Stage Venture Capital

Once you acquire seed venture capital, you're on your way to great success. But you must carefully run your business so that you, and it, are eligible for future rounds of financing from venture capitalists. Keep in mind at all times that what venture capitalists seek is a public offering of your company's stock so they can recover their investment. So:

1. **Run your company in a businesslike manner** at all times. Never splurge on expensive so-called necessities such as lavish parties, a corporate jet, dream vacations for company executives, and the like. Such activities are unnecessary and only detract from your company's reputation and brand.
2. **Follow all accepted business rules** for accounting, human resources (personnel), payroll practices, accounts payable, accounts receivable, taxes, and so on. While there may be a temptation to cut corners, when you want your company to grow with an outstanding expansion record, follow the rules at all times!
3. **Be aware of problems that might arise.** Take action to handle every developing situation early—before it becomes a major challenge and possibly a negative record for your company. Get good legal advice from day one in your company's history. And have a certified public accountant (CPA) do the account books for your company. Then you'll be sure you are in compliance with all business regulations and tax laws.
4. **Treat your employees well.** Build a loyal staff and your company will prosper every day of the year.
5. **Stay in touch with your seed venture capitalists.** One member of the venture capital firm will usually serve on your board of directors. Why? The venture capitalist wants to watch your company to see that it grows steadily and wants to be on hand for your next round of venture financing. I'm sure you'll want a ready advance of cash when you need your start-up venture capital and later rounds of that no-repay money! Having a member of the venture capitalist's firm on your board will ensure quick access by your company to needed funds.

Your Opportunities to Get Venture Capital Are the Best Ever

Count yourself lucky to be reading this book at this time. Why? Because, at the time of this writing, my good friends:

- **Venture capitalists the world over** are scrambling to find promising companies in which they can invest their money. Today I tell people it's a situation in which *too much money is chasing too few deals!* In the old days it was a case of *too many deals chasing too little money!*
- **Millions of dollars are chasing deals** into which venture capital can be invested. And, fortunately for you, there aren't that many good investments available.
- **So if your company has a promising product or service** for which a strong need exists, you're almost guaranteed to get the seed venture capital needed to develop the idea and explore the market demand.

Knowing these facts, you should get to work developing a strong business plan that will attract venture capital quickly. Once you have your business plan, start using the resources listed later in this chapter to get the venture capital you need. With your seed capital in hand, I know it won't be long before you're into the later stages of venture capital, as explained earlier!

Before closing this chapter, you should know that Small Business Investment Companies (SBICs for short), in association with the Small Business Administration, are another excellent source of venture capital for you. SBICs are discussed at length in Chapter 8.

Also, if you decide that you'd like to help small and medium-sized companies raise venture capital, you should get the *Venture Capital Funding Kit* listed in the Appendix. Written by your author, this big kit gives you hundreds of active venture capital firms, dozens of venture capital clubs, and numerous angels you can work with. As part of the service offered to purchasers of this kit, our staff will write, free of charge, the executive summary for your business plan. You can use your executive summary as the first document you send a venture capitalist, a club, or an angel, to interest them in your client's company or your own company.

Your author is your friend. I've associated with venture capitalists for a number of years. They're great people. So listen to what I say because I want you to get the venture capital you seek! I know what turns venture capitalists on. And their turn-ons are in this chapter. So read it carefully and do what it suggests!

Also, over the years I've made personal venture capital investments as well as private loans to some of my newsletter and book readers whose projects are promising. The BWBs receiving this help have been happy with it. Thus, one subscriber-reader writes:

> The business loan you made to me to open my first hobby shop was certainly a help and has given me the chance to open another hobby shop. I thank you very much for the assistance.
>
> *(By letter from Texas)*

Venture Capital Resources for You

Seed Venture Capital Sources

Austin Venture

300 W. 6th St., Suite 2300

Austin, TX 78701

T: 512-485-1900

F: 512-476-3952

www.austinventures.com

Draper Richards LP

50 California St., Suite 2925

San Francisco, CA 94111

T: 415-616-4050

F: 415-616-4060

www.draperrichards.com

Later-Stage Venture Capital Sources

Edison Venture Fund

1009 Lenox Dr., Suite 4

Lawrenceville, NJ 08648

T: 609-896-1900

T: 609-896-0066

www.edisonventure.com

Benchmark Capital
248 Sand Hill Rd., Suite 200
Menlo Park, CA 94025
T: 650-854-8180
F: 650-854-8183
www.benchmark.com

vSpring Capital
2795 E. Cottonwood Pkwy., Suite 360
Salt Lake City, UT 84121
T: 801-942-8999
F: 801-942-8183
www.vspring.com

Venture Capital Clubs
Gold Coast Venture Capital Association
P.O. Box 27-3281
Boca Raton, FL 33427
T: 561-883-2456
www.gcvca.org

Angel Capital Network
1 Harbor Dr., Suite 205
Sausalito, CA 94965
T: 415-289-8701
F: 415-331-3978

Mountain Ingenuity Venture Capital Club
787 Hambley Blvd.
Pikeville, KY 41501
T: 606-432-5504
F: 606-432-7295
www.mivcc.org

Key Ideas for Getting the Venture Capital You Need

- **Venture capital** has many advantages for you and your company, when compared to loans you might secure.
- **Your company must meet** a number of simple requirements to qualify for venture capital funding.
- **Venture capital can be used** to finance the entire growth cycle of your company—from its very start to its full-grown success.
- **Today there are dozens of critical problem areas** for which venture capital is readily available if you have the answer to the problem.
- **Contact venture capitalists** who specialize in your business if you want to speed the results you seek—namely a cash infusion into your business corporation.
- **Start your venture capital financing** with seed money and go on from there to later-stage financing, as you need it.
- **Use your executive summary** as your introduction to seed venture capitalists. A powerful executive summary can be your key to future riches.
- **Create a full business plan** using your executive summary as a guide. Follow the outline given in this chapter for your full business plan. Be sure it is professionally prepared in every aspect.
- **Avoid the sure turndowns** listed in this chapter if you want to raise your seed venture capital quickly and easily.
- **Use a finder, a venture capital club, or an incubator** to help you find and get the seed venture capital you need.
- **Grow your company** so it is eligible for later stages of venture capital that will help you expand and prosper.
- **You're lucky to be seeking venture capital today** because more money is chasing fewer eligible deals than ever before!
- **Use the resources given in this chapter** to find the venture capital you need to convert your ideas into a successful business.
- **You can often find venture capital** through a Small Business Investment Company (SBIC), described more fully in Chapter 8.
- **You have a good friend in your author.** My contact information is in the last paragraph of Chapter 8.

4

How to Get Grants for Your Business

Getting a cash infusion for your business, as you recall from Chapter 3, can be a powerful force in its growth toward commercial success. And a cash infusion that does not have to be repaid can be a lifesaver for you or your business. In this chapter we show you how to find and get valuable sources of cash infusions—namely *grants*—that do not have to be repaid if you do the work for which the grants are made.

In my business, which is financial information gathering and reporting for small businesses of every type, and seeking lenders of money to beginning and experienced wealth builders, grants are a major source of support for a variety of self-employed people and small businesses. Individuals who obtain grants for their work include novelists, playwrights, poets, medical researchers, and so on. Many small businesses receive a major portion of their start-up costs from grants. As a reader of my book, you are my friend. And I'm here to show *you* how to get a grant for *your* business in the easiest and fastest way possible. Let's get started getting you the no-repay money you need.

Know What a Grant Is

A grant is money advanced (paid) to your business to accomplish a stated task. You can get the grant in one of three ways:

1. **As a sole proprietor** in special circumstances—such as a minority, a farmer, a work-at-home mom, a child-care provider starting a business, a creator of an artistic work (a novel, play, poem), and so on.
2. **As a business corporation** awarded a grant to perform a certain task—such as to start a business overseas, research a new medical cure, study and report on transportation facilities, and so on.
3. **As a 501(c) not-for-profit organization** that is organized as a trust, corporation, or another type of approved entity.

Later in this chapter you are provided with sources of information on how your group must be organized to receive grants from foundations.

No matter how you are organized, your business can receive grant money from one of the following: a government (national, state, city, county), a foundation, a large corporation, or a special fund set up to finance companies to accomplish a given task.

Grants have many advantages for your business. These advantages include the following:

- **Once your business gets a grant** and does the work for which the grant was made, more grants are easier to get from the same grantor. (A *grantor* is the organization making the cash grant to you.)
- **Shorter grant application process.** Today fewer and fewer grant organizations require long grant applications. Some grants of as much as $10,000 are made on the basis of a simple two-page grant application.
- **Some grantors today have excess funds** that they must put to work to satisfy their organizers. This means your grants are easier to get today.
- **Grants are available for hundreds of uses.** This makes it easier for your business to get a grant for unique skills, procedures, studies, or other work you might wish to do.

Brush Up on the Many Types of Grants Available

Grants are made for hundreds of different purposes. To help you see the variety of grants that are available, here are some of the more common ones made today:

Broad Categories of Grants

Business—domestic and overseas start-up, expansion.

Real estate—design, construction, purchase, rehab, and so on.

Education—for individuals, teachers, job-loss retraining, and so on.

Health care of many different types for individuals and groups.

The arts—painting, sculpture, music, authors, playwrights.

Under each of these categories of grants there will be hundreds of specialized grants you can apply for and get for your business. For example, here are a few interesting business grants you might wish to apply for in your business:

- **Training of workers** in new, improved skills.
- **Overseas marketing** of food, food products, and related items.
- **Development of energy system** devices, products, and conservation methods.
- **Transportation company start-ups** or expansion—airlines, bus companies, railroads, and so on.
- **Women-operated business start-up**, expansion, improvement.
- **Advanced technology** research and development.
- **Farm and agricultural products** and the conservation of land, water, electricity, and other energy.
- **Ethanol, bio-diesel,** and similar products research and uses.
- **Green design** for buildings, machinery, and other energy-consuming facilities to save fuel.
- **Expansion of** minority-owned businesses.
- **Security systems** at critical utilities—electric power plants, water-supply facilities, sewage disposal—to counteract terrorism threats.
- **Advanced technical** research and development in a variety of important civilian and military fields.

Know the Benefits of Grants to Your Business

You and your company can get the grant money you seek. Grant money you receive for any of the purposes previously listed, or for one of the hundreds of other reasons for which grants are made, is for the estimated expenses of your business activities related to the grant. Organizations making grants to you don't advance money for profits. Instead, grants are made only for your expected costs to perform the work for which the grant is made.

So when you hear grants called "free money," you know the speaker is wrong. Why? Because grant money is *not* free. It is money to cover the expenses that you or your company incur when doing the work for which the grant is made.

So don't turn away from grants thinking they're a waste of time. Grants can get you and your company many beneficial results. Benefits you can expect from the grant money you or your company receive include these:

- **You'll learn how to manage** people, or you'll improve the management skills you already have.
- **You will become a known** (and appreciated) figure at your bank because you'll deposit grant funds and write checks.
- **People will look up to you** when they learn you're doing important work for the country, the city, the county, or your community.
- **You'll meet key people** in your industry—people who may later help you when you're doing for-profit work.
- **You'll become an expert** at putting together business proposals and plans, all of which can benefit you enormously in the future of your own business.
- **You'll have operating funds** for your grant work—perhaps more than you've ever seen in one check at one time!

What Type of Grant Should You Seek?

There are thousands of grants and grantlike cash infusions available to you and your business. So what type of grant should you seek?

You should seek the type of grant that's best suited to your firm's skills and needs.

To determine your firm's skills and needs and the type of grant to apply for, take these easy steps:

1. **Analyze the capabilities** of your firm. What does it (and what do you) do best?
2. **Decide what types of grants** (research, development, production, services) could best match your and your firm's skills.

3. **Assemble information** on your and your firm's capabilities—such as your education, experience, staff you can assemble or call on, and so on.
4. **Check to see if grantors** or similar funding sources are making the type of grant you are looking for.
5. **Develop an action plan** for getting the grant you seek, being certain you can do outstanding work for the organization making the grant to you. Your plan should include the names of the people who will perform specific tasks required in the grant work. Such people need not be your employees. You can outsource this work if it is beneficial for you to do so. Be certain to list the work you will personally do, if you plan to do more than manage the work of others.

See the remaining sections of this chapter for step-by-step data on getting your business grant.

Where Can I Find Grantors?

Grantors *make* grants (give you the money). You, as a receiver of the money, are the *grantee*. These two words save time and space in explaining what you can do to get some of this no-repay money.

Grantors can be found in a number of ways. You can start by doing some research in your local public library and on the Internet. Or you can turn to specialized directories and courses listing grantors and their preferences in making grants. Specific places for you to find grants for your business are:

- **Directories of foundations.** Many are available that list foundations throughout the country. Keep in mind that foundations, in general, make grants only to nonprofit 501(c) organizations. More information on such entities is given later in this chapter.
- **Corporation directories** listing companies that make grants to individuals, businesses, nonprofit organizations, and other deserving entities (schools, colleges, universities, etc.).
- **Federal government data** listing hundreds of grants available to individuals, companies, nonprofits, and local governments. You will find the grants listed in the data published by the various departments of the government—Small Business

Administration (SBA), Internal Revenue Service (IRS), Department of Commerce (DOC), and so on.

- **State, city, and county directories** listing grants for individuals, businesses, nonprofits, and so on. Look on the Internet, or in your local telephone book under "Government."
- **Internet web site searches** for grantors specializing in various types of grants to a variety of grantees. My company, IWS, Inc., will do a free grant search for you if you're a two-year or longer subscriber to our helpful newsletter, *International Wealth Success*. See the Appendix for information about the newsletter.

When searching for grantors you have to use your ingenuity and your knowledge of your business and the skills it brings to the grant. Sometimes you'll find you're the only applicant a grantor has had in months. Why? Because other business grant seekers have not done their homework. If you do your homework in looking for a grantor, you'll be amazed at the amount of grant money you can get for your business. Throughout this chapter we show you how to win in the grant-getting game.

How Do I Apply for My Business Grant?

Following are the specific steps to take to apply for your business grant for yourself or your company. Don't try to shortcut these steps. Why?

In the steps you take in the grant-getting field—sometimes called *grantsmanship*—a two-page single-spaced application letter can get you several hundred thousand dollars in grants. Why try to take shortcuts when the amount of work you do to get your grant is so little? The steps that can be winners for you in getting grants of all kinds for yourself or your business are:

1. **Decide what type of grant** you will apply for—research, development, training, education, or the others mentioned earlier. Without knowing the type of grant you seek, your search efforts can be wasted.
2. **Target your potential grantors.** Prepare a list of possible grantors for your project. Get as many potential grantors on your list as possible. The more potential grantors you have, the greater your chances of getting the grant you seek.

3. **Obtain your tax-exempt status** from the Internal Revenue Service (IRS) if you want to get grants from foundations. You normally cannot get a grant from a foundation if your business is a for-profit entity. You can get details on obtaining your 501(c) status on the IRS web site, www.irs.gov.

4. **Prepare your grant proposal.** If the grantor has a grant application form for you to use (which they will show you in their application data), use the form. Be certain to type every entry in the form. Handwritten grant applications do not win grants!

5. **Submit your grant proposal** to every grantor on your list, if is permissible to make multiple grant applications. Deliver your proposal the way the grantor requests—postal mail, e-mail, fax.

6. **Wait for a positive response.** If your proposal is rejected, don't be discouraged. Submit your proposal to other grantors on your list.

7. **Do the grant work if you're approved.** Be certain to deliver *more than* you promised. Then your grantor will be ready to issue a new grant to you, if your business needs one.

Don't let these steps frighten you. They are simple and quick. Some people can prepare a grant proposal in just a few hours. Your hourly pay for preparing your proposal can be enormous. This is especially true when your grant request is for a large amount of money—in the hundreds of thousands of dollars.

For personal help, as my friend, from myself and my staff of grant experts, I suggest you get a copy of my *Phone-In Mail-In Grants Kit* described in the Appendix. I will personally help you every step of the way in getting your business grant. And my staff assistant, who has worked for years in the grants field, will back me up with wide research for the special grant you need. This service is offered free to users of this kit.

Now let's take a look at each of the steps just listed to see how you can take them all. You'll see that getting grants can be much easier than you might think, especially if you use the kit!

Decide What Type of Grant You Will Apply For

As we saw earlier, you must know something about the subject for which you're seeking your business grant. Thus, let's say you're applying for a grant to

. . . train and educate engineers and architects in the economic design of green buildings to conserve energy while at the same time providing a healthier and safer working and lifestyle environment for the occupants of the buildings.

To get a grant for this training and education activity you, and your company, must:

- **Know something about** green buildings and their design.
- **Have teaching skills** (your own or those of people you hire).
- **Be able to locate** people and firms in the design field.

When you pick such a topic for a grant, you must be well prepared from a knowledge standpoint. Or, if you have just a general background in the topic, you must know or find experts you can call on to deliver the training and education for which your company is getting grant funding.

When you hire experts to do training and education work, the process is known as hiring people and "wrapping a grant" around them. Thus, if you know a little about a topic and sense a growing need for training, education, research, or development about it, you can apply for a grant if you have competent people to perform the task for which the grant is made. You render a service to the grantor by assembling the skilled people to do the needed work.

If you're an expert in some area of technology or science, you can almost certainly get a grant for yourself. All you need do is find a grantor seeking to fund a study or research in your area of expertise.

Write your grant proposal (or have someone write it for you). Send your proposal to the grantors you've picked. A good proposal is almost certain to get you the grant you seek. In summary:

- **Know the field** in which you want a grant.
- **Get to know** the grantors in this field.
- **Tailor** your proposal to each grantor.
- **Keep applying** to grantors until you get your grant.

Target Your Potential Grantors

Here are quick ways to find grantors who might work with you to make the grant you seek. I devised these ways and they are working very well for many BWBs seeking business grants. Using the sources given you earlier in this chapter for lists of grantors:

1. **Phone each grantor.** Ask if they're interested in making a grant of $_____ (the amount you need) for the purpose for which you're seeking a grant. You will get a quick yes or no answer.
2. **E-mail each grantor.** Ask the same question: Are they interested in making a grant of $_____ for the purpose for which you're seeking your grant? Again, you'll get a quick yes or no answer via e-mail.
3. **Write your prospective grantors** asking the same question.

By using what I call my *Phone-in/Mail-in Method*, you can find dozens of interested grantors in a day or so. Once you've found a few interested grantors you can concentrate on preparing a perfect grant proposal that will get you the grant money you need.

So don't waste your time or the grantors' time. Go right to the target. Find out if the work you plan to have financed by a grant is really of interest to grantors. *Remember*: Grantors have specific work they want to accomplish with their money. Offer to do that kind of work and you'll get the money!

To help you get your grant money sooner, I prepared my *Phone-in Mail-in Grants Kit*. People using this kit report great success. You'll find full details about this kit in the Appendix.

To Get Foundation Grants, Obtain Your Tax-Exempt Status

Foundations make grants to tax-exempt organizations. You can easily obtain your tax-exempt status by going to the web site **www.irs. gov** and clicking on the "Charities & Non-Profits" section. You'll find that IRS Publications numbers 557, 3637, and 3755 will be very helpful to you. And they are free for the asking.

If you're not on the Web, you can call or visit your local IRS office. Ask for the three publications just mentioned. They will be given to you free of charge.

While you can form a nonprofit organization yourself, you should have the advice of a competent tax attorney. This will ensure that you comply with the various IRS rules. Again, forming a nonprofit 501(c) organization is simple. You can do the easy work required in a week or less.

Prepare Your Grant Proposal Summary

Many BWBs seeking business money through a grant think that their winning grant proposal must be 500 pages long and six inches thick. Not so these days! When questioned, most people in charge of approving grant proposals and issuing grant checks say:

- **The shorter the proposal**, the quicker the approval.
- **Short proposals** are usually read first, long proposals last.
- **A two-page proposal letter** is often enough to get a tentative yes answer.
- **A grantee (you) who saves** a grantor's time is always popular and is remembered for this trait.
- **Long proposals** may not be as strongly convincing as short proposals.

Recognize here and now that conciseness pays off. Make your proposal short and you may win a large grant sooner. Since you can get a quick answer on the possibility of getting a specific grant, you need just one phone call or letter:

- **Prepare your proposal** in summary form (called an *executive summary*) to start.
- **Use this summary** as the body of your letter, or as your phone-call script.
- **Get a quick yes** or no answer before writing the entire proposal.
- **Expand your proposal** to include more data after you get your "Yes, we're interested" answer.

To show you what I mean, let's say you've decided to apply for a grant to train and educate engineers and architects about green buildings, as mentioned earlier. Your executive summary might then read like this:

> We seek a $500,000 grant to train and educate 100 local engineers and 50 local architects in the economic design of green buildings to conserve energy while at the same time providing a healthier and safer working and lifestyle environment for the occupants of the buildings. The participants in this

training and education will be chosen by the department heads of the engineering and architecture schools at the local state university.

Once you have a tentative approval by a grantor interested in funding this proposal, you can fill in the other key topics in your plan, namely:

- **The need**—why the work described in the grant proposal is needed.
- **What work will be done**—a complete description of what you'll do to complete the goals of the grant.
- **Who will do the work**—information on your staff and its capabilities.
- **How the desired results** will be measured—tests and other statistical targets that will be reported on as the grant work proceeds.
- **How much money** is needed and exactly how it will be used—salaries (including yours), rent, light, heat, travel, and so on.
- **The future**—what other grants might be needed for ongoing work.

Earlier you targeted potential grantors for your project. Now you have your executive summary for your grant proposal. Your next step is to call, or write, all your target grantors, asking if they're interested. Calling targeted grantors on the phone will get you faster answers.

Don't be afraid to call a grantor! Every grantor needs your business to stay in its business! Keep that fact in mind. When calling you can use wording such as this:

Good morning (or afternoon.) My name is _____.
Our organization is _____. We're seeking a $500,000 grant to train and educate engineers and architects in the economic design of green buildings in the area. The grant will be for one year's work on this project. Would you or your organization be interested in making such a grant to us?

You'll get a quick yes or no answer. If the answer is yes, ask the following questions:

1. **"Would a two-page proposal** be enough for you to make your decision?"

    If the answer to this question is yes, say "Good. We'll get the full proposal to you in the next five days."

    If the answer to this question is "We prefer to have grantees use our grant proposal form," say "Please send us a copy via fax, e-mail, or postal mail today. We want to apply for this grant as soon as possible." (As an aside, you may be pleasantly surprised to see that the proposal form is short—sometimes just two pages!)

2. **"To whom** should we address this grant proposal?"

    Make notes of everything you're told during your telephone conversation with the grantor. Be sure to get the correct name, and spelling, of the person to whom you're to send your grant proposal.

If the answer to your question about the grantor's interest in your grant is no, then ask:

1. **"What kinds** of grants are you making today?"

2. **"Who do you think** might make the type of grant we're seeking?"

    Again, makes notes of everything you're told. By doing so you may find one of the grants the organization is making that you can qualify for.

If you'd prefer to write a grantor asking for a grant, instead of phoning, you can use the following sample letter. Call in advance to obtain the name to whom you should address your letter.

Finish Your Grant Proposal Sections

When you get a yes answer, as I hope you do, you will have to complete your grant proposal. If you don't want to write the proposal yourself, you can have someone do it for you. Be certain that anyone you hire has experience preparing grant proposals. This person should have a track record of approved and funded proposals he/she prepared.

Letter Asking a Grantor for a Grant

Date
Grantor Contact
Grantor Organization Name
Address

Dear _____:

We are seeking a grant of $500,000 for one year to train and educate engineers and architects in the economic design of green buildings.

There will be many resulting benefits to the country's energy supply, the cities in which the buildings are located, and to the occupants of the buildings.

We look forward to your response concerning your interest in this grant request. A full proposal is available if this grant request interests you.

Very truly yours,

(Your name and title)

Your grant proposal will have six brief sections that follow your executive summary, outlined earlier. These sections, and a summary of their contents, are as follows:

1. **The Need.** Green buildings are needed to conserve energy, provide better accommodations for occupants, protect against terrorist acts, and conserve construction materials and time.
2. **What Will Be Done.** The grant will furnish funds for the training and education of engineers and architects in the economic design of green buildings of all types—residential, commercial, industrial, and so on. It is anticipated that 100 engineers and 50 architects will receive 12 weeks of part-time training during the first year for which the grant is made. All the trainees will be active designers working in the field. Hence, it is expected that they will quickly incorporate their training and education into their daily design activities.

3. **Who Will Do the Work.** A staff of three competent environmental engineers will conduct training and education on a part-time basis by giving evening classes to the attendees. This staff has wide experience with green buildings and will impart this background to the trainees. Better and safer designs will result.

4. **Measuring Results.** Attendees are all mature professionals. They will be tested every other week during the 12-week duration of their course. The grantor will regularly be sent the results of each test at two-week intervals. A final examination will rate each attendee on his/her understanding of the green building design process. The results of this examination will also be sent to the grantor. Included with the examination results will be an evaluation of each attendee and the overall results of the program.

5. **Money Needed.** A total of $500,000 is needed for one year to cover the salaries, office expenses, travel, group transportation to buildings for on-the-job evaluation of design procedures, and miscellaneous costs. Detailed budgets of each cost are available and will be sent to the grantor on request. Likewise, regular monthly reports of each expenditure will be sent to the grantor.

6. **The Future.** If this program is successful, as the grantee expects it will be, future groups of architects and engineers can be trained in the same way. Further, other areas of the country can be served with similar programs.

You *can* get the type of grant you seek. Your key strategy in applying for any grant, large or small, is this: Don't try to wing it when applying for grant money. Instead, search carefully for grantors making grants for the type of work you do well and like to do. Why? Because one grant successfully accomplished can lead to other grants with quick, simple approval. So apply for grants in areas you (or your staff) know best. Do the best job you can. Finish the work on schedule, and on budget.

Keep in mind at all times that grants are made to help people, either directly or indirectly. You can help people by getting grants for work that's important to citizens of our nation or to people in your area. You and your staff will get a good feeling from doing needed work to help others. And all of us benefit from the work done that's financed by grants!

Key Ideas for Getting the Grant You Need

- **A grant is money** advanced to your business to accomplish a specific task or tasks.
- **Your business must be organized** as a nonprofit entity to receive grants from foundations.
- **Getting nonprofit status** is simple. You apply as detailed in this chapter.
- **Hundreds of different types of grants** are available to businesses to do a variety of good works.
- **Getting a grant offers many advantages** to your business, yourself, and your staff.
- **Seek the type of grant** that best fits the skills of your business and your staff's capabilities.
- **There are many different sources** of information on grantors available to you and your staff.
- **Follow the steps given in this chapter** to apply for the grant you seek for your business.
- **You have a good friend in your author.** My contact information is in the last paragraph of Chapter 8.

5

Raising Money for Your Business by Going Public

You can raise money for your business from the public, or from private investors, by going public. When your corporation *goes public* it sells shares of its stock either on the open stock market or privately to investors through a stockbroker. Your first-time offer to the public is called an *initial public offering* (IPO).

Money you raise through a public (or private) offering is an investment in your corporation. Hence, the money your company receives never has to be repaid. You can use this money to:

- **Buy** a building to house your business.
- **Buy** production machinery for your business.
- **Buy** computers, copiers, telephone systems, autos, trucks, aircraft, and ships for your business.
- **Buy** whatever else is needed to conduct a profitable, growing business.

You can also use the money you raise for many other business activities, such as:

- **Pay** salaries for yourself and your staff.
- **Pay** rent, light, and heat for your office and/or factory.
- **Pay** your travel expenses, and those of your staff.
- **Pay** any other legitimate business expense associated with earning a profit from your business.

The key idea to keep in mind about going public is that the money you raise for your corporation is for business uses of any kind. In getting this money you widen the ownership of your corporation because the outside investors become part owners. You can retain control of your corporation by limiting the number of shares of stock you sell to the public.

Four Easy Ways to Go Public

You can sell stock in your corporation to the public in several ways. The best way to sell stock to the public depends on a number of factors, including:

- **The investment climate** at the time of your public offering.
- **The state of your company**—a start-up with no sales, a start-up plus with just a few sales, a mature firm with strong sales.
- **The reputation** of yourself and your staff in your field of business.

Let's take a quick look at each of these factors to see how it might influence your decisions about going public.

1. **The investment climate.** When lots of new, small companies are going public, the investment climate is good for your offer. The public is enthused about buying shares in new, mostly untried companies. So it's easy for you, and your stockbroker, to find buyers for your corporation's shares. But if the stock market is down or is sluggish, selling shares in new, small companies is difficult. Many companies will hold off going public in such a market atmosphere. And stockbrokers will discourage small-company offers because the public isn't interested.
2. **The state of your company.** If your company has a sales history, it's much easier to go public than if you haven't yet made any sales. But some companies still go public when all they have is debt—that is, money they spent getting started. To go public with no sales but lots of debt, your company must have a breakthrough idea with enormous promise of success. So look for the great idea with lots of potential growth if you're a start-up with zero sales.

3. **Reputation of yourself and your staff.** If you're an expert at some saleable activity, you can go public using your reputation as your key selling point. Or if you've assembled a group of experts in a needed field, you can use their expertise as your reason for going public. Companies go public, and investors buy into them, on the basis of what they can do to generate future sales and profits.

Now that we know what makes people buy into new companies, let's look at four easy ways to go public today. These four ways are:

- **Uniform Limited Offering Registration (ULOR),** also called Small Corporation Offering Registration (SCOR)—sometimes termed a do-it-yourself method.
- **Regulation A** securities offering.
- **Company underwriting** using its personnel as salespeople.
- **Limited partnership** offering to a relatively small number of investors.

Any of these methods can raise the money you need. But the amounts, as we will soon see, vary, depending on the method you use. Your author, as your good friend, is ready to guide you to the best way, in his opinion, to get the funds you need. Other experts may advise you differently. I respect their opinions and recommend that you make your final decision based on the advice from qualified people whose opinions and advice you feel are trustworthy.

If these methods seem a drag, please remember this. When you take your corporation public:

- **Your personal** on-paper wealth can increase enormously.
- **Your company** achieves a certain cachet—it is a public entity.
- **Your corporation** stock can be used to acquire (buy) other companies.
- **Your company's stock** can be used as collateral for loans to your corporation.

The advantages of going public are so great that the usual BWB with a good idea is foolish not to offer his/her stock in the open market!

Are there negatives about going public? Yes, there are. A few of these negatives are:

- **You give away some control** of your company for the money you receive.
- **You have stockholders** who may question your business decisions.
- **You will have to file** certain reports with the government during the year.

True, these negatives may be onerous. But the no-repay money your business receives from your stockholders can make all the pain worthwhile! That's why most BWBs say going public is well worth the effort and the few minor negatives you may meet. Now let's look at various ways you can go public.

Uniform Limited Offering Registration

Also called ULOR and SCOR, this way allows you to raise $1 million a year for your business from the public. So if your business needs more than $1 million a year, skip ahead to the next method of raising money, namely Regulation A, covered in the next section.

To raise money under ULOR, your company must meet certain requirements:

- **Your business must be a corporation** organized under state law in the United States. And you must engage in a business other than petroleum exploration or production, mining, or other extractive industries. "Blind pools" where no specific business is named are not allowed.
- **The securities (stock) sold** can be offered, and sold, only for the named company (that is, your business).
- **Your company's stock** must be sold at $5.00 per share or more. A price of less than $5.00 per share is usually not allowed in a ULOR offering.
- **Selling agents, properly licensed, can sell your stock.** The company (your business) must determine if the agents selling your stock are required to be licensed in the state in which sales are made.
- **Officers of your company** and its selling agents must meet certain requirements regarding their past history with public

companies. You have to read the ULOR Form U-7 for full information on this requirement.

- **Your company cannot raise more than $1 million a year** using the ULOR approach. However, your company can raise $1 million in this way each and every year it is in business.
- **You must file Form D** of Regulation D with the Securities and Exchange Commission (SEC). This is an easy requirement to meet.

Using the ULOR Offering for Financing Your Business

You may say that $1 million a year for your business is not enough. Okay, good friend of mine, wait for the next type of offering, namely Regulation A. Meanwhile, for those other good friends of mine, I want to tell you about the beautiful features of ULOR. These features are:

- **The registration form** gives you a superb outline for an excellent business plan.
- **The registration form** leads you, step-by-step, to a full-compliance document you can use to raise $1 million a year for your business or real estate activities.
- **The registration form** is a simple fill-in-the-blanks type of document that's fun to complete and makes you, and your company, look fully professional.
- **The registration form** tells you what to think about for your business and really leads you to the path for your success.

Let's look at the registration form so you can use it to raise the money you need for your business or real estate. Here are the elements of ULOR Form U-7:

- **Disclosure Document.** This is the first page of your Offering Circular. Here you tell what type of securities you're offering— common stock, restricted stock, notes, bonds, and so on. You also tell the minimum and maximum number of shares you're offering, along with the share price (such as $10), plus the proceeds expected for the minimum and maximum number of shares sold. Thus, your minimum amount might be $500,000, maximum amount $1 million.

You also supply information about who will sell the shares, their commission, and any limitations on the share sale. A prewritten Disclosure Statement telling about the risks of investing in a small business is also included on this page of the ULOR form. Being prewritten, it saves you the time and energy you might spend agonizing over its wording!

- **Table of Contents.** This lists what your registration form will contain when it's finished. And it provides you an ideal outline of what you should have in it.

- **The Company.** Here you fill in the blanks, giving your corporation's name, incorporation details, address, telephone number, and whom to contact at the company.

  Then you list the risk factors faced by your business. Risk factors include cash flow challenges, management's inexperience, unproven products, competition, plus any others that might exist. Again, you enter these in the spaces provided.

- **Business and Properties.** In this section you describe what your business does, or proposes to do. You include what products, goods, or services your business will provide to its customers. Other information you provide includes data on how you will market your products or services.

  Next, you give data on your present employees (if any), and project how many you'll need in the next 12 months. You also give data on the types of employees you'll need—clerical, administrative, management, technical, and so on.

  If your company owns, rents, or otherwise occupies real estate, you give data on the properties. And if the company owns copyrights, patents, trade secrets, know-how, and so on, you give information on these. They are called your *intellectual property.*

- **Offering Price Factors.** Here you give data on the securities you're offering, their price, whether they're convertible to another form, and so on. Any previous sales of your securities are also detailed.

- **Use of Proceeds.** Here's a fun part of your offering. In this section you tell how you'll spend the money raised. For example, if you'll be paying off debt the company incurred earlier, you detail this. Likewise, you give information about items you'll buy for the business, salaries you'll pay the officers (including yourself), and other expenses you expect.

- **Capitalization.** Another good news part, this section tells how much money your company has, and where the money is. You also give details on your company stock shares and any debt.
- **Description of Securities.** Here you tell about your securities, be they common stock, preferred stock, notes or bonds, and so on. This is another fill-in-the-blanks page. Many start-up companies using ULOR offer only common stock to their investors. This simplifies the paperwork and can raise just as much money for you and your company!
- **Plan of Distribution.** Any selling agents are listed here. If you're not using selling agents, then you tell who else might be selling your shares. As a company officer, you are usually allowed to sell shares in your own company.
- **Officers and Key Personnel of the Company.** You give details (name, address, education, qualifications) of yourself and others in your company. This is easy to do because you know most of your helpers well. And you can get them to fill in the details.
- **Principal Stockholders.** This could be you and a few of your associates. You give name, address, and so on.
- **Management Relationships, Remuneration.** If you have any relatives in the firm, that's okay. You tell about it here. And you tell what your major officers are paid.
- **Litigation**. If there are any lawsuits going on, tell about them here. In most start-ups there won't be any legal actions taking place.
- **Federal Tax Aspects.** You tell what kind of taxes you'll be paying. And, good friend of mine, the higher your taxes, the better! "Why?" you ask. Because the higher your taxes, the more money you're making! Never knock having to pay taxes. Why? Because when you're paying taxes it means your business is making money for you!
- **Miscellaneous Factors.** Anything you forgot, put here.
- **Financial Statements.** Your income and expense statements go here.
- **Management's Discussion and Analysis.** Any other good, positive things you want to say about your business, put here. You just answer the questions that are presented on this page and tell about your sales—actual and projected.

While it may seem a chore to prepare your Form U-7, it really can be fun to do. And it will give you a view of your business you may never have had before. So if you start to agonize over the details, just remember what Form U-7 can do for you: *It can put $1 million in your corporation's bank account in a very short time!*

Using the Regulation A Offering Circular

The Regulation A offering circular, shortened to "Reg A" among entrepreneurs, is an SEC document. Note that the SEC is a federal government agency. ULOR offerings are usually governed by state agencies, with the SEC in the background. Using Reg A you can raise up to $5 million a year for your corporation, as compared to $1 million per year for ULOR. Your decision on which way to go public will be based on the annual amount of money you estimate you'll need to carry on a successful business in your chosen field.

Reg A, like ULOR U-7, contains an excellent business plan outline directed at a public stock offering. The elements of the Reg A document are:

- **The Company.** Here you give data on your company—its name, address, your telephone/fax numbers, e-mail address, and person to contact.
- **Risk Factors.** You list, in order of importance, the most substantial risks to investors that your company poses. There are 16 lines for listing the risk factors. But few companies use all the lines.
- **Business and Properties.** In this section you describe in detail what your company does, or proposes to do. Include what products or services are or will be produced, or services that will be rendered. Give data on production methods and new products or services that are planned. Marketing strategies that you plan to use should also be included. You also give data on any orders you might now have on hand. Additionally, any real estate owned, patents or copyrights owned, trade secrets, and other valuable information owned by your company should be listed.
- **Offering Price Factors.** In this section you describe the securities you plan to sell to the public. These will usually be shares of stock in your corporation. You give data on the

offering price, number of shares offered, who will be selling them, and so on.

- **Use of Proceeds.** This is the fun part. You tell what you'll spend the money you raise on—real estate, machinery, employee training, and other company-related expenses. In general, there is no restriction on your spending when you're using the money for the benefit of your business corporation.
- **Capitalization.** Here you give details of what your corporation owes in short- and long-term debt. You also give details of your stock and how it will appear in your corporation's balance sheet.
- **Description of Securities.** In this section you tell about the securities you're selling. You give details on the type(s) of securities you're offering to your investors. Most start-up companies issue only common stock to raise their initial money.
- **Plan of Distribution.** This section tells how you plan to sell your stock to the public to raise up to $5 million per year. It is easy to give this information.
- **Dividends, Distributions, and Redemption.** If the company paid dividends within the past five years, you give that data here. Since most companies have not paid dividends, this is an easy section to fill out. All you say is: "No dividends have been paid in the past five years."
- **Officers and Key Personnel.** Your name will usually be the first on the list of officers and key personnel. You also list the other people who will help you with your business. Include their business qualifications such as their education, previous experience, awards, publications, and speaking engagements.
- **Directors of the Company.** List here your board of directors and their individual qualifications. Follow the example given in Officers and Key Personnel.
- **Principal Stockholders.** Again, your name will be first because as a founder of the company you will be a principal stockholder. List other major stockholders and their holdings of your company's stock.
- **Management Relationships, Transactions, and Remuneration.** You use this section only if you have officers, directors, or key personnel related by blood or marriage. If the company has made a loan to any of these people, you include the details about the loan.

- **Litigation.** If there are any lawsuits against your company, give details in this section.
- **Federal Tax Aspects.** Give information on these matters if your company is an S or C Corporation under the Internal Revenue Code.
- **Miscellaneous Factors.** Cover items you haven't mentioned earlier that are relevant to your company's good financial health.
- **Financial Statements.** Furnish income and expense statements for your company. If you haven't done any business yet, this is an easy section to complete.
- **Management Discussion and Analysis.** Here you round up any financial matters important to the company and its financial statements. Give information on significant sales you may have made in the past year.

Your Challenges When Going Public

The U-7 and Reg A forms may seem onerous when you read the details we've just given you. But that is not so!

If you're enthused about your business and the wealth it will bring you, you'll enjoy completing either of these forms. Further, the very chore of filling out either form helps you see your business as you may never have seen it before.

The questions asked on the U-7 and Reg A forms have been prepared by successful, experienced businesspeople. Answering these questions gets you to the heart of your business. Your answers will help you better understand your marketing, personnel practices, manufacturing, and so on.

For other simple ways of going public, use (1) the SEC form SB-1 if your company is very small; (2) SEC Rule 504 of Regulation D; (3) SEC Rule 505 of Regulation D. These methods allow you to go public easily but you *must* have competent legal and accounting advice to guide you. For helpful information on these methods of going public, go on the Internet to www.sec.gov. Or you can write the SEC at Securities and Exchange Commission, 100 F St. NW, Washington, DC 20540; or call 202-551-6551. For you, as a BWB, the methods given here are among the best you can use at this time.

Do-It-Yourself Public Offering

As an employed officer of your corporation you are allowed to sell stock to the public yourself. The do-it-yourself offering is also called *self-underwriting*. Good ways to do this are with either the ULOR U-7 or SEC Reg A format. You decide which one to use, after analyzing your firm's money needs. (*Note*: When you limit the sale of your stock or other securities to the residents of one state, called an *intrastate offering*, no federal review of your offering circular is required. However, a state review may be required. Your attorney will give you information on the exact requirements.)

Also, when you go public you must be very careful to comply with all the rules and regulations governing stock offerings. To do this, you must:

- **Have the advice** of a competent attorney who is familiar with the SEC and state regulations.
- **Have the advice** of a certified public accountant who knows the rules and regulations governing public offerings.
- **Have the advice** of a brokerage house familiar with small stock offerings. You can both sell shares yourself and have a brokerage house sell shares.
- **Have the advice** of your state securities agency. Why? Because the rules vary from one state to the next. Hence, you must know what rules must be followed in your state.

To see if your self-underwriting would work with investors you can take these easy steps:

1. **Write a short, 300- to 500-word description,** called an executive summary, of your company and the business for which it will use the proceeds of the stock offering.
2. **Focus on the business** your company will engage in. Tell what you'll offer and who will buy your products or services.
3. **Send your executive summary** to several small-issue stock brokerage firms by postal mail, e-mail, or fax. Ask the brokerage firm if they're interested in selling your company stock to the public.
4. **Judge the market potential of your offering** by the reaction of the brokerage houses. If more than one house wants to take you public, you probably have a winner!

To show you a typical executive summary, here is an example from a real-life company that offered its shares itself and through a brokerage house:

Eastern Research Company

The business objective of the Eastern Research Company is to develop new ways to supply nuclear power to local power grids. Since this is a start-up company, no sales have been achieved yet. Management believes that once capital is obtained from this public offering, a significant number of sales can be made to local power companies.

Organized as a (name of State) corporation on Sept. 1, 2____, the company plans to sell one million shares at $5.00 per share to raise $5 million. Members of the management team believe that new opportunities in the power field will become available to the company because of the liquidity provided by the proceeds of this public offering. Decisions as to which new opportunities to research and develop will be made by the company's management. It is possible that such decisions will be made without seeking the consent, vote, or approval of the company's shareholders.

The ability of the company to find new opportunities in its field of business is dependent on the completion of this public offering. Since this is a new business, the company has no operating history. Hence, there can be no assurance that the company will succeed in its plan to supply nuclear power to local electrical grids. Further, the company faces all the risks inherent in the field of nuclear power.

Management members have much experience in the nuclear power field. They expect to find numerous opportunities to apply their knowledge to new business opportunities that may come to the company because of the capital available from this public offering. However, there is no assurance that any of these opportunities will be profitable to the company and its shareholders. Potential buyers of shares in the company should recognize that high risk is involved because the company is still in its start-up stage.

Company Contact: John Jones, Vice President

Address: 123 Main Street, Any City, Any State 12345

Telephone: 324-456-9876

Underwriter: Self and ABC Securities, Inc.

"Why would people ever want to invest in such a company," you ask, "especially after such warnings about the risks involved?" There are any number of reasons people might want to invest, including:

- **The belief** that nuclear power usage will increase.
- **The belief** that the management of the company (listed in the detailed prospectus) has great technical and sales skills.
- **The belief** that this start-up company will become the next Google or Microsoft.

"Further," you ask, "how could any company with no sales history, and only a start-up, go public?" Here's your answer.

Many times, good friend of mine, people will say to you they can't believe that a new, small, untried company without one dollar in sales can go public and raise money. "It can't be!" they say. "I never heard of that!"

Your answer could be, "Just because you never heard of something doesn't mean that it's impossible!" It *is* possible and *does* happen that new, untried companies *do* go public and raise money!

These same people who argue with you often go to their local legal advisers and ask them if it's possible to go public with a new, small, untried company. The adviser, who's intelligent and capable, and great with wills and deeds, usually knows little about going public. But being asked, the adviser pretends to know something and replies: "It can't be done. It's too expensive."

And the BWB believes the adviser, even though the adviser knows little about going public. In the IWS book *Wall Street Syndicators and New Offering Briefs* (described in the Appendix), we give you dozens of excerpts from offering circulars of a number of new and untried firms that have gone public. These excerpts show that:

- **New and untried firms can** and do go public, even though they have yet to make their first sale.
- **There** *is* **a market for stock** of new and untried companies.
- **Many new, untried companies,** *do* raise large amounts of money in the public market when they have a promising idea for a business.
- **The stock can be sold** by the firm itself, or by a Wall Street brokerage house.

So the next someone tells you, "It can't be done," show them a copy of the book just mentioned. It will open their eyes—and hopefully their minds!

Try a Roll-Up Offer to Raise the Money You Need

Some BWBs prefer to buy other companies instead of starting their own firm. These BWBs raise money in an IPO to *roll up* other companies into one large company.

An IPO to buy other companies is sometimes referred to as a *blind pool* because the companies that will be bought are not fully known at the time of the offering. Both ULOR and Reg A prohibit blind pools. Hence, you must use another form of registration to raise money for a blind pool. The usual method used is a full registration with all the disclosure and audit requirements being met. Since the company generally has no sales, and few expenses, the registration is simple to complete.

To be successful with a roll-up blind pool you must have a big idea that grabs investors' attention. Such ideas might be:

- **A cure** for Alzheimer's disease.
- **New ways** to train laid-off workers for productive jobs.
- **Child-care centers** for small businesses.
- **A cure** for AIDS.
- **Ways to** recycle used computers profitably.
- **Faster ways** to recover bad-loan losses.

Once you have such an idea, it is possible to raise money for it using the blind-pool approach. To obtain public money this way:

1. **Develop your idea** in a written business plan that will catch the attention of the public because the results are needed by people facing the disease, lack of work, need for child care, and so on. Include your roll-up ideas for expanding your business quickly.
2. **Convert your business plan** to a stock-offering prospectus similar to the Reg A and ULOR forms. You can get data free from the SEC at the addresses given earlier. (*Note:* You cannot use ULOR or Reg A for a blind-pool offering; you must use the type of registration specified by the SEC or your state securities agency.)

3. **Send your prospectus to a stock broker** who might handle your public offering. Since the income of the stock broker is dependent on the number of public offerings they make, your prospectus will be welcomed.
4. **Follow the advice of your stock broker.** He/she knows what's going on in the market and the best ways to raise money in the current environment.

Follow these suggestions and you can get the money you need using the roll-up and blind-pool methods. Best of all, the money is owned by your corporation to invest wisely as it sees fit!

Use a Limited Partnership to Raise Public Money

Another, simpler way to go public is by using a *limited partnership* (LP). With an LP you have 35 or fewer limited partners who invest in your partnership in the form of *participations*. Each participation can be $5,000, $50,000, $500,000, or any other amount the LP decides on.

An LP is a simpler way to go public because the amount of paperwork you fill out is much less than with a stock offering. But you may be limited to the number of partners you can include in your LP. With fewer partners, each has to put in more money than if you had thousands of people subscribing to your public stock offering.

Limited partnerships are popular for real estate investments. Thus, an LP can be set up to buy and operate one or many of the following types of property:

- An office building.
- An apartment house or residential complex.
- A medical facilities building.
- A hotel, motel, marina, golf course, tennis court.
- Any other income-producing real estate facility.

"What other advantages, if any, do LPs have?" you ask. There are a number of other investor advantages to an LP, such as:

- **Depreciation of the building** in a real estate project can be passed on to its investors. This can help them save on income taxes.

- **Appreciation of a property's value** is shared by its investors when the building or land, or both, is sold.
- **Expenses incurred** by the LP can be spread among the investors, reducing the taxable profit.
- **Operating duties** are carried out by the property employees, relieving investors of the daily management concerns.

To start an LP for your business and raise money with it, take these easy steps, starting right now:

1. **Decide what type of business** you want to raise money for via an LP. You must have a specific business in mind.
2. **Get examples of LP agreements** used to raise money for the type of business you've chosen. You can obtain these from law firms that advised LPs, from stock brokerage houses that handled LP offerings, and from the LPs themselves.
3. **Review carefully each LP agreement.** Choose one that is closest in content to the business you have in mind.
4. **Write your own LP agreement** for your company, using the example as a guide. You'll get the work done much faster by using a successful example to guide your writing.
5. **Take your finished LP agreement to a competent attorney** who knows LPs. Have that person review your LP agreement and revise it, where necessary, so it complies fully with the laws governing LPs in your area. *You* must *take this step. Do not try to sell an LP offering without having full and complete legal advice and counsel. And be certain to follow the legal directions you are given.*
6. **Sell limited partnerships** to investors. You'll find such people at country clubs, golf clubs, tennis clubs, and yacht clubs. Also, medical doctors, dentists, attorneys, and accountants are sources of investment partners—either themselves or their professional associates or family members. Be certain to follow the legal guidelines for presenting your LP offer to investors.
7. **Work at selling LPs until you achieve your money goal.** Typical LPs raise anywhere from $50,000 to $5 million and up. Many LPs raise $250,000 to $750,000. If amounts in this range will meet your company's money needs, then go for it!

You can obtain an example of an actual LP agreements to study from my company, IWS, Inc. This agreement is for study purposes only. It is not offered as a substitute for the necessary legal advice and counsel you *must* obtain from an experienced attorney. See the Appendix for information on these study example forms.

Use a Shell Merger to Go Public

There is one other way you can go public. I didn't mention it earlier because the method is not often used by BWBs. And it can have complications that may cause headaches.

You can go public by merging your corporation with an existing *shell corporation*. Such a corporation is an existing public entity that does no business, but does have public stockholders. And the shell corporation may have capital. Or it may be penniless, having no capital. You will usually pay something—from a few hundred dollars to many thousands—for the shell corporation you merge with. There are several advantages to using a shell to go public, namely:

- **You can go public instantly**—that is, within about two weeks.
- **You may have a much lower cost** to go public when you use a shell than with a ULOR or Reg A offering. (*Note*: In a ULOR or Reg A offering the cost of going public comes out of the money raised, *not* out of your pocket or bank account!)
- **You can use the merged stock** to raise money in the public market.
- **You can take tax deductions** (with the advice of your CPA) on any carry-forward losses the shell may have, after the merger.

But all is not milk and honey! There are disadvantages to your using a shell to go public. These disadvantages are:

- **You inherit any losses** the shell may have—meaning that your corporation will have to pay bills that the shell incurred *before* you bought it!
- **You may find** that there's no—or very little—demand for the shares of stock of your company and its merged shell.
- **You may learn** that some of the dealers handling shell corporations are not the most popular people around. As a result, shell mergers are sometimes thought to be less effective than going public in the traditional way.

You decide how you want to go public. Shell mergers can be successful. But you must be very careful about the shell you pick to do business with. And, as in *all* matters of going public, you *must* have the advice of a competent attorney and CPA *before* making any moves or signing any documents!

Key Ideas for Raising Money from the Public

- **Money you raise from the public** can be used for any normal business need—machinery, equipment, a building, salaries, transportation, shipping, advertising, and so on.
- **There are several easy ways** for you to raise money from the public. The best way for you to use depends on a number of factors: the investment climate when you go public, your reputation, and the state of your company—start-up, growing, mature.
- **You can use any of four ways to take your small firm public.** These are ULOR, Reg A, self-underwriting, and a limited partnership.
- **A ULOR U-7 form is a simple** question-and-answer document that allows your company to raise $1 million a year for its business.
- **Reg A allows your company to raise $5 million a year** for business uses. It, too, is in question-and-answer format but it is somewhat more detailed than the ULOR U-7.
- **Self-underwriting uses either ULOR or Reg A** but has the selling done by corporate officers, or a combination of officers and a brokerage house.
- **A limited partnership offering** is governed by local laws covering these types of securities sales. Hence, you need competent legal guidance.
- **A shell merger is a quick way to go public.** But you *must* be very careful in choosing a shell with which you want to merge.
- **You have a good friend in your author.** You'll find my contact information in the last paragraph of Chapter 8.
- *Never attempt to raise money from the public without experienced, competent legal counsel! You must have such guidance at all times.*

CHAPTER 6

Real Estate Financing Made Easy for You

Income real estate is a popular business with BWBs. And real estate is here to stay! It won't go away. Why? Because we all need:

- **A place to live** that's comfortable and protects us from rain, snow, sleet, hail, and high and low temperatures.
- **A place to conduct our business,** be it an office, a factory, a hotel, motel.
- **A place for sporting events,** recreation, public gatherings, health activities.

Real estate surrounds us every moment of our lives. Even when we're on an airplane, real estate is where our flight started and where it will safely touch down. Likewise with a ship, because we leave one dock and return to the same or another dock. And, good reader friend of mine, real estate will always be with us.

Further, real estate, in my view and experience, is the best way for a beginner to build his or her wealth quickly today. Why? Because:

- **Real estate is a borrowed-money business** from the day you start in it. Financing is at the core of every real estate transaction!
- **You are** *expected* **to borrow money** to start, and expand, your income real estate business.

- **Because it is a borrowed-money business,** you, as a BWB with little or no starting capital, can begin your career using other people's money (OPM). This gives you enormous leverage, allowing you to control large holdings with little or no money of your own.

To show you how you can build a good monthly income on borrowed money, just look at what one of my BWB readers did for himself and his family in a short time:

Quick Real Estate Success

I read your book *How to Make Millions in Real Estate in 3 Years Starting with No Cash* two years ago, and I started using your methods immediately. My first two deals weren't so hot. I was too eager to close and didn't do enough up-front due diligence. But I'll make money on them all the same. These were two small commercial strips in Chicago. I bought them with basically no money down (for one the seller held paper; the other was financed through SBA).

It was on my third try that I really hit a home run. This was an industrial center we acquired through a construction loan. I renovated it, and leased it up within eight months (a year ahead of schedule). For this deal I raised most of the equity money from friends and family, after negotiating the bank down to a 10 percent equity requirement.

So here's where I am at, barely two years after reading your book: Total cost of three properties = $4,670,000; current value based on rent roll = $6,730,000. That's about $7,000,000 worth of real estate bought with only $150,000 of my own money—all borrowed with second and third mortgages on my house. After paying all monthly mortgages (loans) and expenses, I'm clearing about $20,000 a month. Thank you warmly for your encouragement and advice in your books, newsletter, and phone calls.

(By letter from Illinois)

In short, this BWB reader built nearly $7 million in assets (his real estate holdings) plus $20,000 a month in income ($666.66 per day for a 30-day month, or $657.53 per day for a 365-day year), on borrowed money. Most of my readers I talk to on the phone, in person, on the Internet via e-mail, or at my seminars, would be very happy with this size income in a two-year time period.

Starting with proven, successful financing methods, you, too, can build a similar real estate income for yourself. It all comes down to using surefire steps for successfully borrowing for your future real estate wealth. And you can borrow the needed money even if your credit is not the best, or you have no credit at all.

Because real estate is a borrowed-money business, the financing of real estate is a key topic for you and me. And, fortunately, real estate financing is one of the most creative types of money raising known to anyone, anywhere. So let's get you, my good friend, started getting the real estate money you need!

And if none of the creative ways I give you work for you, you can always turn to me personally. Perhaps I can help you—either on a mentoring or private money basis—to get the money you need for your income real estate financing.

Why Real Estate Loans Are Good for You

Real estate, again, my good friend, is a *borrowed-money business!* Few BWBs or EWBs pay all cash for income real estate purchases. Instead, these smart investors use OPM.

If you talk to non-investors (people on a salary who have struggled all their lives to make ends meet), they'll tell you that borrowing is "bad." And they'll add, "Never go into debt. You may not be able to repay the loan you take out."

This is an incorrect belief and wrong advice if the money you borrow is to buy, or rehab, income real estate, since:

- **You are using the money** for constructive purposes.
- **The money you borrow** earns money to repay your loan.
- **Your loan money** will usually grow if you invest it in an active real estate project.
- **Interest you pay on borrowed money** is generally tax-deductible if you use it for income real estate.
- **You leverage yourself** with borrowed money. This means you control a large real estate asset with a small amount of money.

- **Using borrowed money** to leverage yourself is an ideal way for you to build real estate wealth, starting with little or no cash of your own.
- **Result? Borrowed money** can put you on the road to riches in real estate faster than any other method I know of. So borrowing money for income real estate investment is good for you! And it's also good for lenders like myself, and for the economy.

"So," you ask, "what's a good way for me to borrow money for the income real estate I want to buy?" Here are valuable tips for you, my good friend, that can help you get the loan you need quickly:

1. **Have a short business plan** (one or two pages) for each loan application you submit, showing how you will use the money you're borrowing.
2. **Show, in your business plan** exactly how and when you will repay the loan money you receive. Lenders (of whom I'm one) love to see a repayment plan!
3. **Give a specific, detailed listing** showing every date on which you plan to make each loan repayment. If you don't know the calendar date, give the repayment schedule as: "One month after obtaining the loan, make first repayment."
4. **Tell, in your business plan,** how you might be able to repay your loan earlier. Again, give dates for your planned repayments.
5. **Meet with your lender.** Be prepared to make a full presentation of how you'll use the loan money and when you'll make full repayment of the loan. Do this well and you'll get the real estate loan you seek!
6. **Never try to hasten your lender's decision.** The only result you'll get is a no decision. Lenders have their loan approval procedures and they want to follow them. Pushing your lender for a fast decision can upset these procedures. So, for your own success, don't do it! Let the lender decide when to *approve* your loan application and call you in to receive your check, or wire the money to your bank!

As an aside, I'll tell you about my own experiences as a loan officer for a large real estate lender. When I received an attractive loan application that I knew I'd approve, I'd go into another loan officer's office at our lending company and hand him/her the loan application. "What do you think of this one?" I'd ask.

The loan officer would take the loan application, lean back in his/her chair, study it for a few minutes, and then comment on the application.

We'd spend the next 20 or 30 minutes talking over the details of the loan application. Both of us enjoyed this chitchat because it increased our knowledge of borrowers and helped pass the time. Sometimes a third loan officer would join us and the discussion would go on for an hour or so. For us it was lots of fun.

But if the prospective borrower called us and asked us for a fast decision, we'd all yell *no*! Why? Because the borrower was depriving us of our fun time reviewing his/her loan.

So hear what I say and don't try to rush your lender's decision. It will just get you a big *no*!

Is 100 Percent Financing Alive and Well?

With 100 percent financing you borrow all the money you need to buy income-producing real estate. You, good friend of mine, will usually have two loans. One will be for the long-term first mortgage of 15 to 30 years. A second loan will be for the down payment you make on the property. The overall result for you? No money comes out of your pocket or bank account!

People still marvel at 100 percent financing. And perhaps you do, too, my good friend. "Is it possible?" you ask. The answer? *Yes*, it *is* possible and *is* working today! And when I say today, I mean the very day you're reading these words!

For instance, one popular way to obtain 100 percent financing is to buy a building in which you will lease space to one or more tenants having high credit ratings. Then you look for a real estate lender that advertises that it offers up to 100 percent financing for buildings and properties that are *net-leased* to suitable tenants having a high credit rating.

- *Net-leased* **means that the tenant pays you** the normal rent for the property plus certain expenses of the property—insurance, taxes, maintenance—associated with the space that the tenant occupies.
- **A triple net lease means** the tenant pays rent plus taxes, insurance, and maintenance (three charges above the rent) for

the space that you rent to your tenant. These three charges lead to the expression *triple net lease.*

- **It is the lease you have with the tenant** that serves as the collateral for the 100 percent financing because the firm that leases your property has a strong credit rating.

There are other ways for you to arrange 100 percent financing, which permits you to get control of an income-producing asset (real estate) without taking any money out of your pocket or bank account. Meanwhile, the real estate you buy (the asset) repays the loans you take to buy it. Some of these ways are:

1. **Use your (or a partner's) credit-card line(s) of credit** for the down payment on the income real estate. Income from your real estate repays *all* loans, plus expenses, and gives you a monthly positive cash flow (PCF). *You must have a monthly PCF with all income real estate!*
2. **Get the seller to lend you the down payment** via a purchase money (PM) mortgage. Such a PM mortgage serves the same function as the line of credit mentioned in item 1.
3. **Borrow the needed down payment** using any type of loan you can get. Thus, if you already own real estate of any kind, you can usually get an equity loan of some kind on that property. Or you might take a second mortgage on the property.
4. **Bring in a partner who has cash** to put down on the real estate you want to buy. Your partner can either work with you on the real estate or be "silent." A silent partner is repaid over a period of time without being active in the daily operation of the property. Also, your silent partner will receive a share of the profit when the property is sold.
5. **Find a private lender to put up** the down payment you need for the income real estate you want to buy. Your lender has no ownership of the property since you repay the loan fully, on time.

In all these arrangements the real estate itself serves as the collateral for your long-term first-mortgage loan. With real estate in good condition having a PCF, such a first mortgage is easy to get. Thus, 100 percent financing can put you, my good friend, into big money sooner than you think! And I suggest you get started right now. The timing was never better!

Income Real Estate Down Payment Tactics

I've never met a real estate BWB who could not find good income properties to buy. Most BWBs today find *too many* desirable properties to buy. Their main problem is not in finding suitable properties; it is a combination of:

- **Finding the down payment money** needed to take over a desirable property having a strong positive cash flow.
- **Meeting the first mortgage lender's** requirement that the down payment not be borrowed.
- **Being able to repay all loans** on the property and still have a positive cash flow at the end of each month.

How can a BWB meet these requirements? There are several ways to meet them. One of the best ways, which is very popular today, is to **use credit card lines of credit** to supply the down payment cash to take over the property you want. In such case, you must:

1. **Be sure—in advance—that** enough cash will come in each month to allow you to have a positive cash flow from the property. This means that the income from the property pays the first-mortgage loan, your credit card lines of credit loans, plus real estate taxes, maintenance, and any other expenses associated with the property.
2. **Double-check that you have** a large enough income from the property to pay *all* loans (mortgages) and expenses, with cash left over for emergencies. As a lender, I *always* double-check all income and expense calculations on an income property *before* we approve the loan. As they say, it's better to be safe than sorry!

Let's look at a real-life example showing how a BWB like yourself might finance the down payment from his/her credit card lines of credit:

- **Price of income property** = $300,000, with 10 percent ($30,000) down at closing.

- **Income from property** = $57,000 per year.
- **Expenses** (maintenance, insurance) = $9,600 per year.
- **Real estate taxes** = $7,200 per year.
- **First mortgage payment** for a 6 percent, 25-year fixed-rate first mortgage of $270,000 = $1,739 per month, or $20,868 per year.
- **Second mortgage payment** of $30,000 from credit card lines of credit at 16 percent interest for 5 years = $730 per month, or $8,760 per year.
- **Total mortgage payments** = $20,868 + $8,760 = $29,628 per year.
- **Total expenses** = $9,600 + $7,200 + $29,628 = $46,428.
- **Net positive cash flow** = $57,000 − $46,428 = $10,572 per year, or $881.00 per month. After the second mortgage is paid off, the PCF will be $1,611 per month, or $19,332 per year.

Thus, this BWB has a nice PCF for a property he/she took over for no money out of their pocket or bank. Both the first and second mortgage payments come from borrowed money! This income property is paying for itself as the BWB builds riches in real estate while sleeping! The method used here is an excellent down payment tactic for income real estate. Try it yourself, my good friend!

Zero-Down Real Estate Methods for You

Readers call me—again and again—about zero-down real estate. "Can (or does) it really work?" they ask. My answer is, "I have hundreds of real-life letters from readers showing that zero-down real estate really *does* work!" Here are the basic methods you, my good friend, can use to get zero-down real estate:

1. **Zero down,** also called *no money down* and *nothing down,* means that you do not take any money from your bank account or pocket to buy income real estate. I repeat this definition several times because some people seem to need the repetition to understand the concept fully.
2. **Zero-down** income real estate always requires at least two loans: (a) the long-term mortgage (15, 20, 25, 30 years), and (b) the down payment loan that can run from 5 percent to 25 percent of the purchase price. Thus, on a $300,000 purchase price your down payment can range from $15,000

(at 5 percent) to $75,000 (at 25 percent), depending on the amount the lender requires you to put down.

3. **Zero-down** income real estate is easy to get if the property is in reasonably good condition and you can come up with the down payment loan. Why? Because the long-term first mortgage is easy to obtain when a property is in good condition. Your big challenge is always the down payment loan!

To explore the world of down payment loans (DPLs), keep these important facts in mind:

1. **The best DPLs are those** where you do not have to state, in your loan application, the purpose of the loan when you apply for it. Such loans are credit-card lines of credit, home equity loans, second or third mortgages, and so on.
2. **A personal loan can often be** used as a DPL when its purpose combines two or more uses—such as home rehab, debt consolidation, and miscellaneous uses. The *anything* loan, which is made by some lenders, can be used, as the lender says, for *anything*, including a real estate down payment.
3. **The seller may offer you** a purchase money mortgage (PM) for your down payment. This is called *taking paper* for all, or part, of your down payment. Such PM loans usually have a term of three to five years and the interest rate will be about 2 percent higher than you pay for your long-term first mortgage.
4. **Some lenders will offer you 100 percent financing** in a single loan if you have private mortgage insurance (PMI) covering what would be the down payment portion of the purchase price. The PMI will cover anywhere from 5 percent to 25 percent of the purchase price. Cost of this PMI is rolled into the monthly mortgage payment for the property. This can add $100, $200, or more to your monthly payment, depending on the price of the property and the amount the PMI covers. This extra cost may be worthwhile for you if it's the only way you can get 100 percent financing for zero-down real estate.
5. **If you own other real estate property** you can often borrow on it and use the money for your DPL. But you *must*—with any of these loans—be able to pay back the amount owed from the monthly cash flow you get from the property you're

buying. And, good friend of mine, you *must* have a positive cash flow (PCF) from *every* income property. If a property would give a negative cash flow, do *not* buy it!

6. **When you have a bank,** credit union, or other savings account, you can use it as collateral for a *no-stated-purpose loan* (NSPL). You can also use actively traded stocks, bonds, or other paper assets as collateral for NSPLs. I've made private money loans with such collateral. Your interest rate will usually be lower when you have good assets such as these to back up your NSPL.

7. **Relatives who like your real estate** investment plans may be willing to lend you the DPL money you need. Again, you *must* be able to repay in a timely and complete fashion from the income you get from the property you buy.

Here's a recent e-mail from one of my book readers and a subscriber to my IWS *Newsletter,* showing how he's doing zero-down real estate:

I want to thank you for your book *How to Make Millions in Real Estate in 3 Years Starting with No Cash.* I am a living testimony that you can acquire investment properties with no cash down. Over the past year I purchased $4 million worth of investment properties—with no money down. Many times I walked away from the closing with money. I am now in a great position where I can see where my retirement finances are going to come from. I do not have to rely on my 401(k) or Social Security.

(By e-mail from Texas)

How to Get Any Real Estate Loan You Need

Every BWB who wants to get into income real estate who calls me can find good properties. What almost all these BWBs lack is the down payment loan (DPL) money for the property they want to buy. If you're in this situation, what can you do, good friend of mine? Here are your answers:

1. **Decide what type of income real estate you want** to own and get an income from in your spare time.
2. **Look for lenders in your area** who are willing to lend on the type of property you want to own—residential, commercial, industrial, or other.
3. **Prepare a good business plan** showing how the properties you plan to buy and own will earn a profit for you and your lender. While I know that you might regard preparing a business plan as a chore, the rewards for you can be enormous. As a private lender myself, and as a director of a large lending organization, I know that a borrower with a business plan has a much greater chance of getting the loan he/she needs than one without it. When I started out as a loan officer, those loan applications accompanied by a business plan always got my first attention and were often approved the same day they arrived!
4. **Spend lots of time looking for a suitable lender.** Why? Because all you need is one lender and you can be on your way to great wealth. Remember: Your lender must agree with your vision of the real estate empire you want to build for your future wealth. When you find such a lender, its staff can offer you an immense amount of help in structuring your loans so they're easier to repay in a shorter time. The lender's staff may even find attractive properties for you to buy. Why would a lender do this? Because, just like the lending organization I serve, they want to make *more* loans so they can earn more money from their capital! Thus, when we earn more on loans, we can pay a higher interest rate on our savings accounts. Paying higher rates on our savings accounts attracts more deposits to us. This gives us more money to lend for real estate, business, and personal use! Almost every deposit-taking lender thinks and operates this way.

To see how this approach can work for you, here's the real-life experience of one of my readers, who told me about his real estate investing methods. He used the steps I've given to start building his real estate fortune in residential properties. Located in the Midwestern part of the United States, he:

1. **Bought 12 properties in four months** using a local lender who's willing to lend on low-income Section 8 housing.
2. **Concentrated on two- to four-family units** because this is the type of property the lender prefers. Also, the loans on these properties can be insured by the Federal Housing Administration (FHA). The FHA insurance makes the lender more willing to make the loans needed by this reader.
3. **Is able to buy such properties** at 80 percent of their market value because not too many people are interested in them.
4. **Has mortgaged out**—that is, gotten cash back at the closing for each property he bought. These 12 properties have netted him $40,000 in mortgage cash-out in four months.
5. **Makes certain that each property** will give him a positive cash flow before he agrees to buy it.

This BWB looked for lenders for several months before he found one who was willing to work with him. When he found the lender that would finance two- to four-family Section 8 houses, the loan officer assigned to him said, "This is what we can do for you. If you follow our rules and guidelines, we can:

- **Lend up to 85 percent** of the appraised value of the property, provided it is in our lending area.
- **Make your loan quickly** without a lot of paperwork if you prequalify yourself with us by filling out the loan application we give you."

You, too, can do the same in your area. While you may prefer other types of property to own, residential two- to four-family unit buildings are easy to get money for in most areas. True, it may take time to find your lender. But once you do, you can quickly build the real estate wealth you seek.

An Easy Way for You to Get Your Income Real Estate Loan

Talk to any real estate lender, myself included, and you'll learn that our main worry is losing the money we lend. What we lend is called the *principal* of the loan. Thus, if we make a $300,000 mortgage loan, the $300,000 is the principal. Our earnings are the *interest* we charge on the loan, which is much less than the principal.

If a loan goes bad, we're willing to lose the interest on it to get our principal back. Losing the interest hurts, but not as much as losing the principal. Why is this? Because we have to bring in at least $10 in sales to free up $1 to loan out. So if we lose $300,000 in principal, it represents about $3 million in sales! That's a big number for any lender. So keep in mind at all times:

- **The principal is the biggest part of any loan** since it's the money we have to advance to a borrower to close a loan.
- **The interest, especially on short-term loans, is a lot less** than the principal. Since interest is the money the lender can earn on a loan, it can be replaced if the principal is recovered and the lender puts the principal out again on another loan.

To keep your real estate lender happy, you have to provide some way of insuring that the principal loaned to you will be returned to the lender in the event you default (that is, not repay) on the loan. The way for you to do this and make it easier to get real estate loans is to **get private mortgage insurance (PMI)** from one of the companies offering such insurance for real estate loans. This type of insurance is also called lender's mortgage insurance (LMI), so you may hear either term when talking to your lender. The advantages of doing this are:

- **This insurance is available at low cost today** (about $300 per $100,000 of loan amount covered). You may be able to negotiate a lower cost.
- **It guarantees your lender** either that a portion of the principal will be repaid in full or that regular monthly payments will be made in full to the lender. The remaining principal is recovered with the sale of the property after it is reclaimed from the borrower.
- **It removes any doubt your lender may have** about being able to get the money back if there is a problem with the loan.

To make getting your loan easier, contact a few private mortgage insurance companies as soon as you have an idea of how large a mortgage loan you'll need to get the kind of property you want to buy. Then:

- **Ask for the insurance papers that are used.** Carefully look over these papers to be sure you can meet whatever requirements are in them. The papers are usually simple to fill out since the insurance company relies on the value of the property to cover the loan amount.

- **Once you find a suitable property,** contact a lender and tell the loan officer that you've checked out private mortgage insurance and believe you can cover the loan with it. Most PMI will cover 20 or 25 percent of the loan because the lender depends on the sale of the property to get back the remaining portion of the loan they made. Ask your lender if they will accept your loan application with the PMI. (*Note*: PMI practices may vary in your area. So be certain to check with local PMI companies to verify the coverage they offer.)

- **As soon as a lender says yes,** contact the insurance company from whom you received the paperwork by sending them a filled-out application for private mortgage insurance. If you've picked a good property, there's an excellent chance your insurance will be approved. As soon as your application for PMI is approved, contact your lender immediately, stating that you have the needed insurance for the loan. If you work with any of the major insurance companies, your real estate loan should get final approval in just hours.

So remember: PMI *can* help you get your income real estate loans more easily. Why not start now?

Use Hard-Hat Money for Your Real Estate Project

If you develop real estate by planning and building (or using a contractor to build for you) projects of various kinds (multifamily apartment houses, shopping malls, townhouses), consider using hard-hat money now.

- *Hard-hat money* **is funds** put into a project while it is still in the planning stage. So the people putting money into the project are called hard hats—that is, they're in the project when it's being built, as are hard-hat construction workers.

- **You can raise millions of dollars** this way for your real estate project using a limited partnership that is sold to the public. Thus, one firm raised $35 million for a project using this method of bringing investors into the deal during planning. You can do much the same for your project.
- **To make the hard-hat method work,** you need to know a few secrets that big money raisers use. Once you know these secrets you can look for big money for your real estate project.

The keys to getting real estate money the hard-hat way are the same for every project, namely:

- **Bring your investors in early,** when the project planning is just starting. This gives investors a feeling of control—they have a say in the planning steps of the real estate project.
- **Show investors how their money can grow** from the moment they put it into the real estate project until it is finished. Thus, in a typical real estate project, the value of $1 invested can, for example, grow to $3 by the time a project is put up for sale.
- **Point out that big money-raising savings result** with the limited partnership method since the money comes into the project in big chunks—typically $5,000 to $100,000, or more, per investor.

Firms organized as a limited partnership are easy to form. And they can cost less than a corporation to form. But if you plan to sell shares in your limited partnership, either to the public or privately, you *must* have the help and guidance of an experienced attorney. Do *not* try to cut corners on this step. You *must* have competent legal counsel!

What kinds of real estate get the most money from these hard-hat offerings? Apartment houses, garden-type single-family home developments, shopping malls, industrial parks, sports complexes, and similar projects get big money the hard-hat way. So if your real estate ambitions turn to planning and development, put on that hard hat and get your money!

How to Overcome the Down Payment Blues

BWB real estate investors have said to me, at least a thousand times, "I can find great properties. But I can't find any down payment money. What can I do?" If this question is *your* question, you can:

1. **Use your credit card line of credit** as a source of the down payment money you need. With lines of credit reaching as high as $100,000 for corporate credit cards, you have a ready source of quick money. What's more:
   - **You're never asked** what you're using the money for.
   - **You get your funds** in just hours with no waiting.
   - **Your interest cost** is tax-deductible for business use.
   - **You can time your receipt** of the credit card funds with the real estate closing, so your usage does not show up before the closing.
   - **You can use funds** from more than one card to build up the cash for your real estate down payment.

2. **Get a personal signature loan** from a financial institution of some type—bank, credit union, savings and loan, building and loan—for your down payment. Personal loans are made for hundreds of different purposes. Speak to a potential lender *before* applying for your loan. Ask the lender for a list of the types of personal signature loans they make. Then see if you can match your need to one of the types of loans they make.

3. **Have the seller take back a mortgage** on the sale of the property to you. The seller is lending you the down payment that you need to take over the real estate. You can work such a deal when:
   - **The seller** is anxious to sell and get out of the property.
   - **The seller** likes you and wants you to have the property.
   - **The seller** seeks an installment sale for tax reasons.

   One of my readers, a good friend such as yourself, told me he is working at taking over a 20-unit apartment house priced at $695,000 with a first mortgage of $525,000 from a lender. The seller is taking back a mortgage of $170,000 (a purchase money mortgage) for the down payment, repayable monthly over seven years. So the buyer gets into the property with zero cash. He will refinance the property in 6 to

12 months to get cash out to either reduce the PM mortgage or rehab the property.

4. **Find and use a cosigner** to improve your credit rating with your prospective lender. This will help you get a down payment loan. Why? Because every lender seeks borrowers with a strong credit rating. Using a cosigner can improve your overall credit score enormously, even when your score is strong at the start. Having a stronger overall credit rating (you and your cosigner) never ever hurt a borrower! The stronger the better, from a lender's view. How do I know? I'm director of a large lender, and have made loans privately myself. We're delighted to have a strong-credit cosigner on any loan we make! Why? Because it makes us feel safer. And every lender enjoys feeling safer!

5. **Have your seller take out an equity loan** against the property for the down payment. You assume the responsibility for repaying the equity loan. Your seller has cash for the down payment, you have the property, and everyone is happy. It's a win-win situation. If you don't repay the equity down payment loan in full, the property goes back (reverts) to the seller. All payments you made on the down payment loan are credited to the seller.

You *can* overcome the down payment blues! Use any of these five methods for your real estate deal. For the property you buy, you may have to alter these methods slightly. Every situation is different in one way or another. The main key for you is to keep trying different methods. You never know when the method you suggest will be accepted by the seller and you'll be in the deal in just hours! Never give up!

Lastly, *work the numbers*! You *must* be able to make *all* loan payments and pay all the expenses of the property and still have a positive cash flow (PCF) every month, and for the entire year. And, as you know, good friend of mine, I'll work the numbers for you free of charge if you're a subscriber to one of my newsletters, listed in the Appendix.

Keep in mind at *all* times:

> **Real estate is a *numbers* business. It *always* comes down to the *numbers* in real estate! So get comfortable with real estate numbers. They can make *you* rich!**

Real Estate Down Payment Strategies That Work

You can find great properties that have a strong positive cash flow. But, as with many other real estate BWBs, you:

- **Don't have the money** needed for the down payment on the property—typically 10, 20, 25 percent of the selling price.
- **Can't figure out how to get** the needed money for the down payment.
- **May have bitten off more** than you can chew by trying to buy a property that's too large for a starter investment.

How can such BWBs get the down payment money they need? Here are six ways to get the down payment you need, good friend of mine:

1. **Convince the seller that you're the best person** to take over his/her real estate. Make the seller feel safe and secure in dealing with you. Become the seller's best buddy and confidant.
2. **Work the age difference,** if you're younger than the seller, which you probably are. Convince sellers that they are doing a good deed by helping a younger person get started in the great business of real estate.
3. **Pay the asking price.** Make sellers feel that they got the best price possible. Let sellers feel that they are sharp wheeler-dealers who are also expert negotiators. Convince sellers that the great deal worked because you, the ambitious young empire builder, are sitting at their feet drinking in the know-how they have to impart to you! Be modest, unassuming, and anxious to learn at all times. It will pay off in better deals for you and your loved ones!
4. **Agree to *all* terms the seller proposes,** if the terms do not reduce your income from the property. Be cooperative. Never fight with sellers! Go along with their terms. Show admiration for their skill, know-how, and wise evaluation of the real estate market.
5. **Ask the seller, in view of your great cooperation** in paying the asking price, to reduce—or eliminate—the cash down payment needed. Explain that you've fallen in love with the property (actually it's the income from the property that

you've fallen in love with!). Tell the seller you will take as good or better care of the property than he/she has. But point out that you're cash-short and just need this one *big* break to get started.

6. **Get the seller to cosign** on a down payment loan for you. Agree to pay it off quickly, using the income from the property.

The older the seller, the easier it is to work zero-down cash deals for real estate. Why? Because older sellers are usually in a rush to get out from under their property. Also, they listen to and admire younger people who are ambitious and know their goals in life. You can get the real estate you want by convincing sellers that you're the right person for them at the right time in their lives!

Ways to Get 100 Percent Commercial Financing Today

People ask, again and again, "Can I still get 100 percent financing for commercial real estate?" The answer—happily—is *yes*, you can! Here's how:

1. **Start by knowing that 100 percent financing *is* available** for office buildings, stores, shopping malls, and similar commercial structures.
2. **Lenders offer from $1 million** to $25 million, and much more, to buyers of various types of commercial real estate when the property produces a positive cash flow after paying *all* expenses, including the long-term mortgage and any down payment loan.
3. **If you and your business will occupy** more than half the space in a commercial building, you can get 100 percent financing from $500,000 up to $5 million, or more, at good interest rates.
4. **Medical facilities**—such as outpatient offices, medical suites, dental offices, and similar buildings—can easily get 100 percent financing. Loan amounts go up to the amount needed for design, construction, and outfitting the building.

Commercial buildings are often a joy to own and operate because you're dealing with businesspeople. Your tenants recognize that they need your space to earn their livelihood. Hence, they pay their rent on time, are patient with you when they ask for repairs, and expect rent increases as time passes. So you'll find that commercial tenants are much less emotional than residential tenants. That's why some of my good-friend readers specialize in commercial properties and find them a joy to own while building their riches in real estate!

Money for the Asking for Income Real Estate

Money *is* available for your income real estate deals from many different sources. You can tap into these sources if the income property you're considering buying shows a positive cash flow. Sources you should check in your local area, and nationally, include:

- **Property equity loans** on real estate you own now (also called home equity loans) can provide cash for your down payment on additional property you want to acquire.
- **Second mortgages on property** you currently own can likewise provide down payment money. And on some new income property the seller might be willing to take a second mortgage as your down payment. You must—of course—have a positive cash flow after paying all expenses, including your mortgage loans.
- **Form a limited partnership** to raise money to take over income property. Some limited partnerships raise as much as $50 million for real estate.
- **Get together with several** friends and have them take equity loans on their real estate. Pool the money received and invest it in larger income properties than any of your friends could buy by themselves.
- **Watch your daily newspaper and Internet real estate pages,** along with the *IWS Newsletter*, for properties advertised for zero down. Sooner, or later, you'll spot a good property that has full owner financing. When you see it, jump at the chance to acquire it—if it produces a positive cash flow!
- **Remember that the income property** you buy is 70 to 90 percent of the collateral you'll need for your income real estate loans. So all you'll need to raise is 30 percent, and possibly only 10 percent, of the price of the property. And that's

easy when you use any of the methods we give you here, my good friend!

Borrow from a Lender Who Knows the Property

Before a lender will lend you money on a real estate property, the value of the building and land must be determined. Your lender will ask for an appraisal of the property to determine its *fair market value.*

The key to your getting the real estate loan you seek is to find a property that will be acceptable to your lender. If you are willing to deal in less-than-prime-condition property, consider repossessed properties—also called *foreclosures.* With these properties:

- **The lender who repossessed** (took back) the property from its previous owner is often willing to lend again to a new buyer.
- **The lender knows the property** but still wants to get it off its books. What we lenders call *real estate owned* (REO) property looks bad on our books because it means we made poor lending decisions. Regulators chew the lenders out for such decisions. (As the director of a successful large lender, I've been on the receiving end of a regulator's ire, and I can tell you it's no fun when a government representative finds you at fault!)
- **REO properties can be sold without the need** for your having an inspection, appraisal, or other reviews because all of this was done by the lender as part of the foreclosure procedure.
- **Zero-cash-down deals** are often possible for you, my good friend, because the lender knows the property and wants to get out of it quickly. We hate having REOs on our books!
- **In some cases we pay your closing costs,** giving you a full no-money-down deal for an income property that can get you started in your real estate wealth building. Some lenders will even have their legal staff do the needed closing work free of charge.
- **And we lenders get you the loan you need** quickly, easily, and with none of the hassle that some BWBs face when trying to finance their first few income properties. Again, we want to unload REOs as quickly as possible.

To show you how easy it can be to get your real estate financing from a lender who knows the property, here's a recent letter from a reader that explains it all:

The bank just accepted my offer for the income property I told you about on the telephone. Comparable properties appraise at $607,000; the property I'm buying is an REO listed by the bank at $399,000. The bank agreed to pay 100 percent for closing costs. So, like you said, I can buy with instant equity and zero down. And that's exactly what happened! I just had to pitch in $3,000 for earnest money that will be returned to me at closing.

I thank you so much for the motivation. I would not have thought of doing this if I had not read your books and I had not talked to you on the phone. I bought two of your books in August, subscribed to your newsletter, and started acting on it right away. It's only been a month and I'm looking at instant equity. [About $208,000, figured by your author.] There's still some upgrade work to do on this property. But I was assured I can get rehab money fairly easily.

(By letter, from Washington)

This letter shows everything I've been talking about when you get a quick, easy loan from a lender that has repossessed a property by foreclosing on it. The reader's property is an REO that needs some rehab work. The lender paid all closing costs, and there is instant equity (ownership) for the buyer. This reader, a woman in the state of Washington, received over $200,000 in instant ownership in less than a month! And she can borrow against this equity to rehab the property and/or to buy other income properties. So this method of getting real estate funding really does work! And, good friend of mine, it can work for you. Just try it!

Get a Down Payment Grant for Income Real Estate

In trying to get income real estate, your biggest challenge will be finding the down payment money. One of the most common questions I get on the phone is, "I found a *great* property; now how and where do I get the down payment money?"

This chapter has already given you a number of ways to get your down payment money. Now I want to give you more ways. One of the best ways for BWBs to get their down payment money is to **get a down payment grant** from a suitable grantor in your local area, or in a distant area. Down payment grants are made by:

- **Local neighborhood improvement groups** that want to see better housing in their area—either in the form of new construction or the rehabbing of existing housing.
- **Historic restoration grants** made by an organization or government to preserve an historic structure you plan to buy.
- **Patient or senior-care grants** made to help the ill or elderly live a better life in clean, neat housing.
- **Homestead groups** that encourage multifamily home ownership to provide suitable housing for inner-city people by making down payment grants (or loans) to ambitious multifamily owners.
- **Home-ownership groups** made up of builders and lenders that encourage first-time home buyers by providing down payment grants. These grants can be for both single-family and multifamily homes. And some of these organizations will make loans to people other than first-time home buyers— such as builders, developers, and similar organizations.
- **State governments throughout the United States** almost all have a down payment grant program for first-time, and later-time, home buyers of both single- and multifamily homes. You will find these listed in my book, *How to Acquire $1 Million in Income Real Estate in One Year Using Borrowed Money in Your Free Time*, listed in the Appendix.

My staff and I regularly monitor down payment grants because there are so many requests for this kind of funding from the readers of my two newsletters. We supply, free of charge, a list of down payment grantors to any subscriber to either of our newsletters who requests this information. A number of our subscribers report they have successfully obtained down payment grants for their income property purchases.

"Why is a down payment grant so important?" you ask. Such a grant is so important because:

- **The property you're buying** serves as anywhere from 75 percent to 90 percent of the collateral for your first mortgage loan. Thus, for a $400,000 property, you would get a $300,000 first mortgage at 75 percent loan-to-value ratio (LTV), or $360,000 at 90 percent LTV.
- **You must now find** $100,000 for your down payment with the $300,000 first mortgage (that is, $300,000 first mortgage + $100,000 down payment = $400,000, the price of the property), or $40,000 with the $360,000 mortgage.
- **Most BWBs have trouble finding enough money** for their down payment. So if they can get this money from a grant that never has to be repaid, the BWB can buy the property sooner and have a larger positive cash flow from it every month. That's why down payment grants are so important! Down payment grants can be your lifeline to success in real estate.

Acquire Income Real Estate for Less Than $100 in Financing

Up to now in this chapter we've been looking at income real estate loans in the conventional money range—$100,000, $500,000, and so on. But there's a section of real estate in which you need less than $100 to take over an income producer. Here's how you can get in on this part of real estate, my good friend.

To find really low-cost income real estate that you can acquire quickly with little hassle, and that you can run almost automatically:

1. **Look in vacation areas** of the United States—Florida, Arizona, Colorado, California—where older people move after retiring from their job or business. These people are:
2. **Buying low-cost housing**—such as a trailer, motor home, or mobile home. Their goal is to keep their mortgage payments low because they're on a fixed income and don't want to have to make large monthly payments.

3. **Seeking a home** with at least two bedrooms (room for the kids to stay when they visit), plus a living room, kitchen, den, and bathroom.
4. **Furnishing the trailer, motor home, or mobile home** with all the conveniences they had in their former home—TV, computer, satellite dish, hi-fi, VCR, Internet wireless, and so on.
5. **Preparing to live their golden years** in comfort and convenience because "you deserve it," as their kids tell them. (Secretly, the kids hope their parents won't spend too much of the expected inheritance!)

The retirees move in and enjoy their purchase. All goes well until some event upsets the apple cart—usually illness, an accident, death, or some other catastrophe. Then they want to get rid of the trailer, motor home, or mobile home in a hurry because the financial burden of keeping the dream home is just too great.

This is where you come in. How? You take easy, low-cost steps in your spare time to acquire income real estate at a very low price:

1. **Visit trailer, motor home, and mobile home parks** in areas where retirees congregate. Do this by driving to the actual areas. Or you can visit many of these areas via the Internet on your computer.
2. **Ask for the manager or owner.** Tell that person you're looking to buy a trailer, motor home, or mobile home at the lowest possible price, and that you're ready to pay cash.
3. **Expect to visit 10 or more sites** before you find your first zero-down, $100 price trailer or motor home. Don't give up—these properties *are* out there and *are* available to you. The only requirement is that you keep looking!
4. **Take over desirable properties** immediately after you know you can either rent or flip them at a profit. Don't delay. Some of these properties are so cheap—costing only $1—that they are snapped up instantly.
5. **Rent out or flip the property** as soon as you acquire it. Your rental income must be at least $150 per month more than the ground lease monthly payment. Be certain to get a security deposit—at least two months' rent—to protect you from problems. *Remember:* Even if you plan to flip the property,

having a paying tenant in it and a security deposit in the bank will help you get a higher flip price for the property!

To show you how this system works, here's a real-life example from a reader in Florida. She told me she took over a two-bedroom, fully furnished 41-foot, four-year-old trailer fully equipped (towels, dishes, sheets, large-screen TV, small TV, VCR, and so on) for $1.00. The reason she was able to do this was:

- **She was on the lookout** for zero-cash opportunities in the Florida area.
- **She found an owner** who had health problems and could no longer use the trailer and wanted to get rid of the lot rent of $293 per month.
- **She had only one other expense** associated with the trailer: A $44 registration fee had to be paid. So for $45 this BWB got a beautiful trailer home she could rent immediately for $600 per month. From this she will pay the monthly lot rent of $293, leaving her $307 per month profit from the trailer.
- **She was offered one trailer** free of charge during her search for such investment properties. But its condition wasn't good enough to justify the cost of rehabbing it. So she turned it down for the $45 trailer!

This reader BWB told me: "I decided to approach real estate financing from the buying end, instead of looking for lenders. And I found a niche market where the properties are almost given away. This eliminates the need to seek outside financing! That makes getting into income real estate on zero cash a lot of fun, and very, very profitable!"

Knowing what you now know, why not look at getting one or more rental homes that can make you rich on zero cash, or nearly zero cash? Here are the steps to take to ensure you get rich using this approach to income real estate finance:

1. **Know in advance** that you can rent the trailer, motor home, or mobile home for at least $150 per month over the lot lease. If you can get more than $150 per month, great!
2. **Check with local rental agents** *before* you buy any of these units to verify that there is a rental demand for them. Find

out what rent you can charge for the unit based on its size, location, and amenities. If you plan to flip the unit, get information on the going prices and typical length of time on the market before the unit is sold.

3. **Always demand a positive cash flow** from each unit you buy. Do not get yourself into a losing deal. Refuse to buy any unit that will have a negative cash flow!

4. **Do not take over the payments on a trailer,** motor home, or mobile home if they are so large you're forced into a negative cash flow. You may be told the unit is free but it really is not! Its cost is the monthly payment times the number of months left on the mortgage. Thus, $210 per month payment for 35 remaining months equals $7,350. That's not *free*!

5. **A typical income and expense statement** for a trailer might be:

Monthly rental income to you	$600
Montly lot lease	$293
Net monthly profit ($600 − $293)	$307
Annual monthly profit (12 × $307)	$3,684

Get 50 of these trailers at under $100 each and your yearly profit comes to $184,200. Not bad for an essentially zero-cash investment with no loan hassles!

Note again, good friend of mine:

Real estate *always* comes down to the numbers! So get comfortable with numbers. They contain *your* future wealth!

Key Ideas for Getting Your Real Estate Loan

- **Real estate loans are good for you** because they help you acquire valuable assets while your credit rating improves and your wealth grows.
- **100 percent financing is alive and well today** for BWBs seeking to acquire real estate for their future wealth. You, too, can use 100 percent financing in your wealth building.
- **There are many useful tactics you can use** to get the down payment for your income real estate. Such tactics can be used by anyone wanting to buy income real estate.
- **Zero-down real estate methods can help you** get income real estate without taking money out of your bank account.
- **There are many ways** for you to get any real estate loan you need for the income property you want to buy.
- **You can use easy ways** to get your income real estate loan, speeding the results you seek.
- **Hard-hat money** is a unique way for you to get the real estate financing you need.
- **You can overcome the down payment blues** by using a number of smart techniques to get the down payment money you need for the income real estate you want to buy.
- **There are a number of ways you can get 100 percent financing** for commercial real estate today. Use the ones given to you in this chapter, my good friend!
- **Equity loans, second mortgages,** and a variety of other methods can be used to get money for the asking for income real estate.
- **Borrow from a lender who knows the property** that interests you, and your loan will be approved much sooner!
- **Down payment grants for income real estate are available to you.** This means you can get 100 percent financing without ever having to repay the money.
- **You can acquire income real estate for under $100**—if you know where to look for it and can follow simple directions.
- **You have a good friend in your author.** You'll find my contact information in the last paragraph of Chapter 8.

CHAPTER

7

Proven Ways to Get Asset-Based Funding You Need

Asset-based funding is any financing where you use some type of asset—such as a home, an office building, undeveloped land, a ship, an airplane, a business, or equipment used in a business—as collateral for the funding. In this chapter I give you a number of methods you can use to get asset-based funding of many different types.

Asset-based funding is highly desirable for BWBs and EWBs, because not only can you get long-term financing, you can also earn quick short-term profits. Here are two letters from readers showing how asset-based financing can lead to quick profits:

> I bought a $165,000 duplex that was fully rented, "paying" zero cash down, and made $5,000 at closing.
>
> **(By letter from Texas)**

What these two readers did was to use the inherent value of financed assets—in this case real estate—to earn money quickly. Their earnings, in each case, were based on the value of the financed asset they controlled. You, too, can do the same for either long-term finance or short-term profits.

> I was able to flip the contract on a 57-unit
> apartment building to another investor for a
> $65,000 profit, before expenses. The seller
> will get back $164,000 at closing. It was your
> book, time, and availability that allowed me
> to do it.
>
> *(By letter from Ohio)*

So let's see how you can get control of an asset and use it for your funding or profit needs.

An important point I want to make to you right now, before we go any further is this, my good friend:

All you need is *control* of an asset to make money from it. You do *not* need to own it!

A Simple Way to Get Financing of Zero-Down Assets

Zero-down funding can come in many different forms. The simplest form of zero-down funding, in my view, is the *down payment grant*. Such grants were mentioned in Chapter 6. Here is more helpful information for you that will enable you to get a down payment grant based on the business or real estate asset you want to acquire.

A down payment grant is money advanced to you to acquire an asset—usually real estate. Down payment grants are less common for buying a business because:

- **Many businesses** have few hard assets (such as land, machinery, a building, valuable equipment) that can be used as collateral.
- **Many businesses** do not have an ongoing management team that can continue the organization if the buyer is no longer able to operate it.

Down payment grants are made by most states in the United States. To get full data on down payment grants made by your state, contact your state housing agency and business development agency. Both are good sources of free information on down payment grants available to you. You will find a full list of these agencies in my book *How to Acquire $1 Million in Income Real Estate in One Year Using Borrowed Money in Your Free Time,* available from the publisher of the book you're reading and from my firm, IWS, Inc. See the Appendix for details.

Down payment grants can be obtained for both single-family homes and multifamily properties. So you can use such a grant for either your personal residence or a rental investment property. There are also grants for starting or buying a business. Again, check with your local agencies for details on such grants.

Getting a down payment grant for an investment property or a business gives you zero-down ownership of an income-producing asset. You take no money out of your pocket or bank. This is one of the best examples of asset-based funding because the real estate or business is the asset on which both the down payment grant and the long-term first mortgage are based.

The beauty of your down payment grant is that you never have to repay the money you receive as a grant. Hence, you can get a monthly positive cash flow from your income real estate or business much more readily. Why? Because you make just one mortgage payment each month for your first, and only, loan on the property or business.

Down payment grants are also made by groups of builders and lenders who want to encourage home ownership. The down payment grants made by these groups are for both single- and multi-family home properties. My firm, IWS, Inc., does ongoing research of these down payment programs in which we keep updated lists of such grants. The list of current down payment grant programs available from nonstate groups is free of charge to two-year subscribers to either of our newsletters listed in the Appendix.

Use Options to Control Assets Until You Sell Them

When you control a valuable asset with little money of your own, you're said to be using *leverage.* You can use an option contract to control valuable assets with very little outlay of money on your part. What's more, that money can be borrowed, so you're using 100 percent financing. You're getting your asset-based funding using just a piece of paper and a few dollars in cash! Let's see how you can use options in your wealth building.

You can take an option on almost anything of value that other people might want to acquire. Thus, you can use an option to control, for a stated period of time (30 days, 60 days, 180 days, and so on), any of these types of assets:

- **Real estate** of all kinds—residential, commercial, industrial.
- **Machinery** for printing, manufacturing, computing.
- **Aircraft** of all types—passenger, cargo, law enforcement, fire-fighting.
- **Ships**—passenger, box freighter, tanker, oil-field service.

Options are common in real estate transactions because land and buildings are freely bought and sold every day of the week. Further, the assets—namely the land and the structure on it—are understood by every experienced wealth builder.

Likewise, options are used to control, for a stated time, assets in the form of machinery, aircraft, ships, and vehicles of various types. If you're familiar with any of these kinds of assets you can finance them with paper and earn good fees selling the items through traditional ads in printed publications, on the Internet, or via a network of dealers in the type of asset you have on hand.

To help you get asset-based funding using options, let me show you the essence of earning money from options with some simple techniques.

Write a Protective Option

Write your option, or have an attorney write the option for you, so you are protected in every way possible. Thus:

1. **Have a 6-month** to 18-month life to control the asset you plan to sell. The longer an option runs, the better for you.
2. **Word your option contract** so the seller who grants you the option (called the optioner) continues to make any monthly payments associated with the asset you're optioning. These payments could be for the mortgage, taxes, heating, maintenance, and so on. Likewise, the seller will continue to receive any income from the optioned asset (such as rents, lease payments).
3. **Pay for your option using cash,** a promissory note, or with a pledge of any other valuable consideration such as stocks, bonds, savings accounts, certificates of deposit, and so on. You can thereby control a valuable asset with no money out of your pocket, because the cash can be borrowed. Make every

effort to keep the amount you pay for the option as small as possible. Why? Because if you do not *exercise* (that is, *use*) the option and it expires, the amount you paid for it reverts to the seller of the option.

4. **Advertise the asset for sale** in places where you have the greatest chance for a fast turnover. This could be in the Sunday newspapers, in magazines serving a specific field (real estate, aircraft, shipping), on the Internet, or through associations unique to the field of the asset (apartment owners, airlines, shipping companies).

5. **Remember that no specialized license** is required to sell an asset on which you have an option. Hence, you have great freedom in this field of financing.

6. **Be certain to have *every* option** you prepare reviewed by an attorney familiar with the field of the asset (real estate, machinery, aircraft, marine).

Examples of Real-Life Options

Following are two examples of real-life option documents. These are given only as examples and should not be used in actual transactions without first being reviewed and approved by a competent attorney.

Real Estate Option

_____ (Seller's name) hereby grants _____ (Buyer's name) the right to purchase the property detailed below:

_____

_____(Give full property data as listed at the County Clerk's office) at a price of $_____ for the next 90 (ninety) days from this date. The Buyer will pay the Seller the total sum of $_____ for this right. In the event this Option is not exercised by the Buyer within the stated time period of 90 days, the sum paid to the Seller by the Buyer will be kept by the Seller and the right granted herein will cease. At the end of the Option term, this Option can be renewed if both parties agree to do so. Agreed:

_____ Seller _____ Date

_____ Buyer

_____ Date

Machinery Option

_____ (Corporation's Name) hereby grants
_____ (Buying Company's Name) the right
to purchase the following machinery:
_____in a where-is and as-is con-
dition for the next 180 (one hundred eighty) days from this date. The
Buyer will pay the Seller the sum of $_____ for this right. In the event
this Option is not exercised by the Buyer within the stated time period of
180 days, the full sum paid to the Seller by the Buyer will be kept by the
Seller and the right granted herein will cease. At the end of the Option
term, this Option can be renewed if both parties agree to do so.
Agreed:

_____ Seller

_____ Date

_____ Buyer

_____ Date

These simple options can be modified if the seller and buyer
agree. Typical modifications include:

- **Fixed option:** The price of the asset named in the option
  remains the same for the life of the option. Thus, if the price
  is $500,000, this price stays the same from day 1 to the final
  day of the option.
- **Laddered option:** When an option has a long term—say
  six months or more—a laddered option may be used. With this
  type of option the price of the asset will rise at stated intervals—
  say every three months. Thus, with an 18-month option and
  a $500,000 sales price, the price might rise 10 percent every
  6 months. So at the end of the first 6 months, the price of the
  asset would become $550,000; at the end of 12 months, $605,000.
- **Credit-back option:** With this type of option the full amount
  you paid for the option is credited to your purchase price
  when you exercise the option—that is, buy the asset. Thus, if
  you paid $5,000 for the option to buy the asset at $500,000, your
  payment at closing would be $500,000 − $5,000 = $495,000.
- **Reduced-credit option:** With this type of option, the amount
  you're credited back declines as the life of the option

lengthens. Thus, with the $5,000 cost previously mentioned, this might decline to $2,500 (one-half) after the option life is half over. Such a clause is intended to motivate the buyer (you) to exercise the option quickly, to save money.

Real-Life Option in Action

To show you how you can use an option to control and finance the purchase of an asset, here's a real-life example of an option at work.

Let's say you know printing machinery, having worked in the field for a number of years. You hear about a large four-color press that's for sale for $1.2 million. Shortly after hearing this, a friend of yours tells you he's looking for a good buy on a four-color press for his business. You tell your friend you think you know of such a press that can be purchased at a bargain price.

You contact the seller and tell him that you'd like a 60-day option on the press at a price of $1 million. The seller counteroffers a price of $1.1 million. Since you think you can sell the press for $1.2 million, the original asking price, you agree to the $1.1 million price. You and the seller sign a 60-day option similar to one of those described in the preceding section. You pay $1,000 for this option, which you borrow on a personal loan.

Next, you contact your friend, the printer looking for the four-color press, and tell him you have an excellent machine available for $1.2 million. You send him the technical details of the press. After studying the technical details, your friend says he'd like to inspect the machine. You arrange for the inspection of the press, after which your friend offers you $1.15 million for the press. You agree to this price because you've made a quick sale and haven't worked too hard while you controlled the asset, namely the printing press. Here's how your numbers work out:

Your sales price	$1,150,000
Your purchase price	$1,100,000
Your gross profit	$50,000
Your option cost	$1,000
Your other costs	$800
Your net profit	$48,200
Your total working time	10 hours

So for 10 hours' work on this option deal where you finance and control a valuable asset ($1 million-plus) with little money ($1,000), you have earned over $48,000! This is another example of how you can use asset-based funding to build your wealth.

You can use the same approach with real estate. To do so you take these simple steps:

- **Find a real estate property** you think you can sell at a profit once you have control of it.
- **Get control of the real estate asset** using an option, as previously described. Try to get your option at the lowest cost for the longest time.
- **Sell the property** as quickly as possible at the highest price possible, once you have the option. This is called *exercising* your option.
- **Go on to** your next option deal.

Mortgage Out and Get Paid for Financing an Asset

People ask, again and again, about mortgaging out on a business or real estate deal. "Can it really be done?" they ask. Yes, it can, and you can mortgage out!

Mortgaging out is a real estate or business transaction in which you acquire an asset of value and receive money at the time you gain official control of the property or business (called *taking title to* or *closing on*). Mortgaging out is also called a *windfall*.

Mortgaging out can occur in several different ways for business and real estate transactions:

1. **Use an assumable mortgage and an asset-based loan.** In this type of transaction you take title to a business or real estate property by accepting the obligation to make the remaining payments on the existing assumable mortgage on the property or business you're buying. Your down payment can come from a property improvement loan or an inventory loan you get. For a property-improvement type of loan you use the

property you're buying as the collateral for your down payment loan. For an inventory loan, you use the inventory of the business you're buying as the collateral.

For example: You buy a four-unit multifamily property:

Price of property you're buying	$500,000
Assumable mortgage on property	$400,000
Down payment required	$100,000
Property improvement loan from another lender	$150,000
Closing costs	$8,000

You mortgage out with $150,000 less $100,000 down, less $8,000 closing costs, for a total of $42,000.

In addition you will receive the rent security deposits for this multifamily property that equal $18,000. Thus, your total mortgaging-out cash received for financing a valuable asset comes to $42,000 plus $18,000, for a total of $60,000. This is cash in your bank! (*Note:* You cannot, of course, use the $18,000 rent security deposits, because local law requires that these funds be kept in escrow until the tenant moves out of the apartment he/she rents. However, your bank will be happy to hold these funds safely for you. And the bank will regard you as a favored depositor!)

2. **Use a mortgage assumption clause** when the existing business or real estate property mortgage is not assumable. You assume responsibility for making mortgage payments on the asset, and get another loan to finance the down payment, using the business or real estate asset you are buying as collateral. Again, you are getting asset-based funding at zero out-of-pocket cost to yourself. You mortgage out when your down payment loan exceeds the amount needed, and you collect rent security deposits for real estate, or business accounts receivable to you as owner.

3. **Have the seller take out a loan on the property** or business to cover the down payment plus additional miscellaneous expenses that always seem to pop up. You assume responsibility for repaying the down payment loan, the seller has his/her cash, and you mortgage out with the difference.

Add to this any rent security deposits, inventory, or accounts receivable and you have your mortgaging-out money. The cash you have can be used as collateral for an additional loan you may need.

4. **Get the seller to cosign with you** on a loan for the down payment plus other expenses you expect, using the business or real estate as collateral. Your mortgaging-out money is the rent security deposits, inventory, or accounts receivables (money owed to the business you're buying.)

5. **A buyer's change of mind** about an agreed-on purchase price can at times lead to mortgaging out without the buyer ever expecting it to happen. Thus, take the case of an agreed-on sale price of $500,000 for a building and a business you want to buy. You get a signed loan commitment from a lender for $450,000 for the building and business. But you get worried about the deal, call the seller and say, "I'm really worried about this deal. In fact I'm so worried, I've decided to call it off. So I suggest you find another buyer." The seller, wanting to close the deal quickly, says, "Well, how much would you be willing to pay?" You reply: "The most I'll pay is $400,000." And the seller says, "You've got a deal!" The deal goes through at the lower price and you mortgage out with $450,000 less $400,000, for a total of $50,000, less closing costs and other expenses.

When you mortgage out you *must* be sure your income from the business or property will cover *all* your loan payments. Plus, you *must* have a positive cash flow from your purchase *every* month of the year! So work your numbers carefully. And, as a subscriber to one of my newsletters, I'll be happy to work the numbers for you free of charge.

Use Debt Assumption for Your Financing

Sometimes you can go into debt to get your financing. While this may seem a strange way to acquire assets, it can be your best source of quick, no-hassle acquisition of assets. What I'm talking about, good friend of mine, is using an assumable mortgage to take over real estate or a business. Assumable-mortgage income property and business takeover deals are great for you because:

1. **You get the property or business** with no credit check, no credit investigation, no financial reviews.
2. **You take over the property or business,** and its income, without ever filling out a mortgage application.
3. **You can concentrate on getting** the down payment money because the long-term assumable mortgage is already in place.

And keep in mind that an assumable mortgage offers you all of the following advantages:

- **A loan on a property or business** obtained by someone other than you, using their credit rating.
- **A loan (mortgage) obtained at an earlier date**—before you ever made an offer to buy.
- **A loan you take over with no change** in its terms—interest, monthly payment amount, term (number of years for payoff)—regardless of current rates.
- **A loan you get without the lender ever investigating** your credit rating, without ever asking how long you've been on your present job, without your being asked what you and your spouse earn.
- **A loan on which you just start making monthly payments** when you buy the property or business. The lender doesn't care whose name is on the payment check so long as it comes in on time and in the correct amount. And your monthly payments come from the real estate or business you buy—not out of your pocket!

When you get financing using debt assumption you put yourself in the winner's circle quickly because:

1. **You can get a large loan** without having to qualify for it using the traditional standards. And you can raise your net worth quickly and easily without any hassles.
2. **You can get your loan,** even with shaky credit. Your credit score won't get in the way of your taking over profitable real estate or a strong, growing business.
3. **You will never be turned down** for having too many inquiries on your credit report. Why? Because with an assumable mortgage there are no inquiries made on your credit report!

4. **You can take over** one property or business after another with no one saying you're expanding too quickly.

Debt assumption can be your key to financing the business or real estate you want. So start looking for takeover prospects having an assumable mortgage. It could be your path to financing the real estate or business of your dreams! And, as a subscriber to either of our newsletters, I'll help you analyze, free of charge, any assumable mortgage you want to take over. Use your assumable mortgage as shown in the first example in the previous section of this chapter.

Get Business Asset-Based Loans in Just Hours

You can use a lender to give you a loan in just 48 hours for work your business has completed for a large corporation, a university, a hospital, or a local or national government. This type of loan is called an *accounts receivable loan* because it is based on money owed to you for work you've completed for one of these types of organizations. You are borrowing on the work you've finished—which is an asset worth the amount you're billing for it.

The lender making such a loan is called a *factor*. A factoring lender making an accounts receivable loan to you or your company will usually lend you 80 percent of what you're owed within 48 hours of submitting your bill(s) to it. Thus, if you've completed $100,000 worth of work, you'll receive $80,000 within 48 hours of submitting your bills to the factor.

The reason companies use factors is because some large organizations delay paying their bills. It can take 30, 60, 90, or 120 days for small companies to receive payment for work they've already finished for large organizations. Meanwhile, the small firm has to pay its staff, pay its suppliers, and pay its rent. This is where the factor comes to the rescue. The factor pays within 48 hours so its client company can continue business as usual.

You can use factoring in either or both of two ways:

1. **As a source of funding for your company** that does work for large organizations in either your local area or a distant area. You will get your funding quickly and dependably. Your only cost is interest on the money advanced to you from the time you receive it until the time your factor collects on your bills.

This could be a week, a month, or three months—but almost always less than a year.

2. **As a source of income for yourself, or your firm,** when you act as an independent contractor representative or finder for a factoring firm that will pay you a commission for each borrower you find who receives a loan. Most factoring firms will pay you an ongoing commission when borrowers you find continue to receive loans in the future. So you'll have what some people call residual income for years if your clients continue to use the services of the factor.

My company, IWS, Inc., has referral relationships with two factoring companies. One of these companies is on the East Cost; the other is on the West Coast. Both these factors welcome users of our *Small Business Loan Kit*, described in the Appendix. Call them on their toll-free number and tell them that Ty Hicks sent you from his kit, and they'll welcome you with open arms. You'll have your loan, or be an official agent, in a short time.

The commission you'll be paid by a factor can vary with the amount of the loan and the industry it is in. Some factors (also called accounts receivable lenders) pay a commission of 2 percent of the amount of the loan, plus a closing bonus of 1.5 percent of the amount of the loan. Your commission would be $3,500 on a $100,000 factoring loan.

Factoring lenders can be independent funders set up to issue accounts receivable loans. Or they can be commercial banks that have a factoring department. When you act as a factoring agent you do not normally need a license because you operate under the factor's license.

Factoring comes back to the asset—the completed work—that has been established by you, your company, or another organization. And the accounts receivable loan is made on the basis of that asset as your, or your client's, collateral for the loan. Further, the credit rating of the large organization for which you did the work also backs the loan.

Make Cash-Flow Notes Your Source of Funding

Cash-flow notes are pieces of paper representing assets of some type that usually deliver regular monthly payments to the holder of the note. The payments may be made for many different reasons, such as:

- **Settling an estate** in which the receiver of the payments is an heir or beneficiary of the estate.
- **Sale of a business** for which part of the payment is in notes.
- **Purchase of real estate**—a home or income property—with part of the sales price being a purchase money (PM) mortgage on which the home seller receives monthly payments.
- **Proceeds of a lawsuit** for which payments are made over time.
- **Lottery payments** made to a lottery winner over a number of years.

In any cash-flow note, two people are involved, the note seller and the note buyer. The note itself is backed by an asset of some kind, such as one of those just listed. This asset can be a source of funding for you when you act as a cash-flow note finder and bring the seller and buyer together. For example:

- **A businessperson sells a business** for $100,000. The person buying the business puts $25,000 down and agrees to pay the balance of $75,000 at 8 percent interest over a five-year period in monthly payments of $1,521.
- **One year has passed** and the seller of the business needs cash. He/she offers the remaining 48 notes (60 months minus 12 payments made by the business buyer) for sale. The value of these notes is $73,008. The business seller is now a note seller.
- **You find a note buyer** who offers $47,455 (65 percent of the 48-month value) to the note seller through you.
- **Your note buyer** will receive $73,008 over 48 months and will earn a profit of $25,553 over four years. This is a return of about 14 percent, which is much higher than they could earn at a bank.
- **You, as a cash-flow note finder,** earn a nice commission (which can be as high as 5 percent of the note price) that is pure money—no big expenses attached to it! You can use your commission as your financing for this, or another, business. And best of all, you *never* put up any of your own money when you raise funding with cash-flow notes!

Turn Paper into Cash for Your Funding

Turning paper into cash is a good way for you to raise the money you need for your business or real estate deals. To put us both on the same page, let's define *paper:*

> **Paper** **is any document that can be substituted for cash** that gives you the same result as putting up cash for business and real estate transactions. The paper is, or represents, an asset that can back the funding you need.

Typical paper that you, a partner, or an investor in your business might turn into cash to help with the funding you need for the business includes:

1. **A contract you or a partner** hold that pays you, or your partner, a certain amount per year to supply a product or service.
2. **A lease on a real estate property** that gives a stated positive cash flow income of a known amount every year—such as $10,000, $50,000, $100,000.
3. **A line of credit** from a bank, a credit card company, or another financial source.
4. **A letter of credit** from a bank, finance company, insurance company, or other financial institution that can be used as collateral for a loan.
5. **An equity line of credit** for the ownership portion you or a partner have in real estate or other valuable assets.
6. **A promissory note** you or a partner have from a borrower, stating that a certain amount of money will be paid to you over a named time period.
7. **A lawsuit settlement** guaranteeing payment of a named amount of money over a stated number of months.
8. **A purchase money mortgage** you or a partner received in place of cash when you sold a piece of property.

To convert any of this paper to cash for your funding needs take the following easy steps, knowing that the paper represents an asset that can be the collateral for the funding you need:

1. **Figure out how much money** you need, and for what purpose. Round off the amount you need to a commonly used number— for example, round $98,400 up to $100,000.

2. **Contact a suitable lender.** Don't waste your time on lenders who *might* make a loan. Focus on lenders who make the type of loan you need for business or real estate.
3. **Ask the lender you've chosen** if it accepts the type of paper collateral that you have and are offering.
4. **Get the lender's loan application** and fill it out, using a copy of it as a worksheet. Be sure to type every entry, except your signature!
5. **Send a copy of your paper collateral** with your completed loan application, along with a one- or two-page business plan showing how you'll use the money you're applying for.

Paper can be your savior when you need a business or real estate loan in a hurry. Review what paper you have available now and see how you can use it!

Use an SBA Loan to Get Your Funding

We mentioned Small Business Administration (SBA) loans in Chapter 1. Here's more info on getting these easy-to-get asset-based guaranteed loans. The SBA offers guarantees on a variety of business loans. You owe it to yourself to check what's available and how you might use an SBA guarantee for your asset-based business or real estate loan.

Some BWBs avoid the SBA guaranteed loans, saying "There's too much paperwork!" Wrong! Why? Because:

1. **SBA uses streamlined paperwork** so you have fewer sheets of paper than with many other lenders.
2. **SBA speeds its decision time** so you get a fast answer on your loan request—sometimes in less than 48 hours.
3. **SBA guaranteed loans** give you the same money as you'd get from other loans. And always remember: *Your goal is to get your loan!* Any legal approach that works is good for you.

Keep in mind that SBA does not make direct loans. Instead, SBA guarantees repayment of your loan to the lender who makes the loan to you. Because an SBA guarantee is solid gold, many more lenders are willing to work with you than if you don't have a guarantee. The guarantee acts as your asset! To obtain an SBA loan:

- **Consider getting an SBA loan for $50,000** or less. Why? Because your SBA loan application for such loans is very short—just one sheet of paper, front and back. It's called the 4 (8-01) Short Form.
- **Apply for an SBA-guaranteed loan** for either a new or existing business. Loans are made for either type of business. So you really can get started sooner using this asset—the guarantee!
- **SBA guarantees real estate loans** if the property you're buying will be used in a non–real estate business. Thus, SBA will advance money for a machine-tool business needing a factory building to house its machinery.
- **Submit with your loan application** your Personal Financial Statement, SBA Form 413, and your Statement of Personal History, Form 912. Both are easy to fill out.
- **Send your loan application** to a lender of your choice, once you've typed it fully. The SBA estimates it takes 0.7 hours (42 minutes) to fill out its short loan application form. Why so little time? Because the SBA simplified the loan application form to the point where you, good friend of mine, can quickly fill it out. And we strongly suggest that you *type* the loan application, instead of writing it in longhand! Typed apps get quick attention. I know. I was a loan officer at a large lender for many years before I became president and chairman of the board. A typed loan application always got my immediate attention. And I approved more typed apps than handwritten ones!
- **Pick your SBA lender from local banks** you'll find in the Yellow Pages and on the Internet. Today many such lenders can make their loan decision without having to contact the SBA. Such lenders are authorized by the SBA to make on-the-spot lending decisions. This speeds your loan approval.
- **If you need more than $50,000** for your business, get an SBA form for such a loan. It's Form 4-L (8-01), Long Form. It, too, is simple and fast to fill out.
- **Contact SBA by phone** at the office listed in your local phone book. Or go on the Internet to www.sba.gov and download their forms and instructions. Yes, SBA can be a great asset for you and your business loans! While you're on the SBA site, check out their microloans, 7(a) general loans, 8(a) loan program, disaster loans, export loans, and 504/503 loans.

Raise Money for Business or Real Estate on Little Cash

Raising money for business or real estate on little cash is easy if you know how. And here's how:

1. **Form a mortgage fund** as a limited partnership to invest in mortgages on good business and/or real estate deals.
2. **Get investors to put money into your mortgage fund** in amounts of $5,000 or more each.
3. **Have an experienced attorney** prepare your limited partnership agreement based on the type of business or real estate you want to invest in. (You can get copies of typical limited partnership agreements from IWS to use as a guide to what you want to say in your own agreements.)
4. **Figure out how much money you need** for your mortgage fund. You should be looking for at least $500,000 to $1 million. Beyond that you should use a real estate investment trust (REIT) to raise money for real estate. For business, use a Regulation A stock sale. Resources for all these are listed in the Appendix.
5. **Get lists of investors to whom you can promote your business.** You can find such lists at major mailing-list houses. Follow the rules of your local and national authorities when contacting investors. Your attorney will outline these for you. Just be sure to do exactly as you're told.
6. **Deliver a high rate of return** on the money invested in your mortgage fund. Be sure that you can deliver what you promise. Thus, if you promise an 8 percent return to your investors, you should earn at least 10 percent. Why? You need a cushion in the event your earnings fall one year.
7. **Have an accountant and attorney on call** at all times to answer any questions you or your investors have. These professionals will help you operate your mortgage fund properly so you obey all the rules that apply to it, fully and completely.

A mortgage fund can get you business/real estate money quickly without too much work. But you *must* have competent legal and accounting advice along the way. The fund pays the cost of the professional advice you require.

Find Bridge Loans and Grow Rich

A *bridge loan* is money you get to cover (bridge over) the financing of one project (an asset) before another asset is funded. Thus, a bridge loan (also called *interim financing*) can be used for covering:

- **The down payment** on a property or business (the asset) you want to buy before you sell a property or business (another asset) you already own. You will pay off the bridge loan when you sell your current property or business.
- **The down payment** and rehab cost of a property or business you want to buy, upgrade, and flip to earn a big profit.
- **The down payment** on land you want to buy and build on, using construction financing you get because you control a desirable asset.

There are many other creative ways you can use bridge financing. The nice things about bridge financing are:

- **You usually** make no payments on the bridge loan while you have it because the interest is due when you repay the loan.
- **You usually** are not subject to an in-depth credit check for a bridge loan because the property serves as most of the collateral you need for the interim financing.
- **You usually** can get a bridge loan faster than a long-term mortgage because the shorter term of a typical bridge loan (one to three years) leads to faster approval.

"So where can I get a bridge loan?" you ask. Bridge loans are usually made by the same lenders that make long-term mortgage loans. Also, bridge loans are sometimes made by lenders specializing in business loans. Thus, you can get bridge loans from:

- **Long-term mortgage lenders**—banks, mortgage brokers, insurance companies, and so on.
- **Commercial banks** making traditional business loans.
- **Credit unions** of many types and sizes.

To get a bridge loan you *must* ask for one. Be exact and take these steps:

1. **Have a specific property or business** you want to acquire; know everything you can about it, particularly the money numbers.
2. **Ask for the amount** you need for your bridge loan, rounded up to the next typical amount. Thus, with $98,200 needed, ask for $100,000.
3. **Tell the lender you want a** *bridge loan.* Your chances of getting it are best when you ask for a bridge loan for a specific deal!

Use an Equity Club for Easier Asset-Based Financing

Let's say you, a friend, or a client need money to invest in real estate. But those needing the money don't have the best of credit, or they don't have any cash. What can be done? Here's a powerful asset-based method that works because real estate is one of the best assets for lenders. They love to make real estate asset-based loans. So you:

- **Form an equity club** for local real estate investors needing money to get started, or to expand their holdings.
- **Limit membership** to people who own real estate in which they have equity (that is, they have paid down part of their mortgage while the price of the property has risen). Their equity in the property is their *asset* for the asset-based loan the club will get. For example, an owner who still owes $200,000 on a building with a market value of $500,000 has an equity of $500,000 − $200,000 = $300,000. The owner can borrow at least $300,000 on that equity because it's a solid asset for the loan.
- **Tell the members** that they will pool their equity to raise cash for the down payments on income real estate. Have an attorney draw up suitable agreements for the pooling of assets.
- **Hold meetings in which** you review the members' equity holdings and decide what real estate they'll invest in.
- **Take an equity-holding position** for yourself if you're the organizer of the club and do the work of scheduling meetings, notifying members, getting the meeting place, and so on. Your equity could be 5 percent, 10 percent, and so on, depending on how much work you do for the club, its members, and the investors.

- **Find suitable properties** that meet the member's income and growth goals. Get the needed data on each property (price, income, expenses, down payment) for your members.
- **Have selected equity holders tap into** their equity when they find—with your help—a suitable property. You will receive a portion of ownership (say 3 percent, 5 percent, etc.) for your work. Or you may prefer a commission for your work. This gives you an immediate asset that will look great on your financial statement.
- **Build a series of equity investments** using the goals, ideas, and funding of the club members. You, as manager, help your members reach their goals with the counsel of local real estate agents, an attorney, and an accountant. Never go ahead with your club or any investments without the advice of competent professionals you pay from club membership dues.
- **Figure your potential part-time income** from running the club by estimating how much might be invested the first year, second year, and so on. Thus, if $500,000 equity money is invested for the down payments on three properties and your share is 5 percent, you'll receive $25,000 in either ownership or commissions. Your second year could be double this, part-time. An equity club is a great way to get your financing on zero-cash investment by yourself.
- **Soon, your equity will help you get the loan** you seek for your own business or real estate investments. Meanwhile, you've received the income and experience that only such a unique club can give you.

To Pay Lower Interest, Try a LIBOR-Based Loan

When a lender asks for a high interest rate, say any amount more than 8 percent, to finance your business or real estate assets, consider a LIBOR loan. This type of financing is defined as follows:

A *LIBOR loan* is funding based on the London Interbank Offered Rate (hence the name LIBOR). The LIBOR rate is keyed to the interest rate international commercial banks pay when they borrow from each other. More and more U.S. lenders are offering LIBOR-based loans for business and real estate.

So what advantages do you have with a LIBOR-based loan using the assets of a business or real estate? There are a number of advantages for you, namely:

1. **You can get an interest-only loan** for a 10-year term. This reduces your monthly loan payment to just the interest on the amount you borrow. Hence, you have more cash available each month from your business or real estate. (Smart BWBs set aside some money each month to meet the eventual principal payment you must make, if you don't sell the business or real estate before the loan payment date.)

2. **The LIBOR interest rate** may be lower than the rate you'd pay that's based on other standards.

3. **Some LIBOR-based loans** have a monthly adjustable interest rate. This can save you money when interest rates are down. Other LIBOR-based loans can have a six-month adjustable rate. Such rates can help you earn more money from the business or real estate you finance with a LIBOR-based loan.

4. **Using a LIBOR-based** low-interest/interest-only loan you might make payments for a year or two on it, and then refinance at a later date to take tax-free money out of the business or real estate, after either has risen in value.

To find a LIBOR-based loan, check the IWS monthly newsletter, *International Wealth Success,* your local newspapers, and other business publications.

Put a Compensating Balance to Work for Your Loan

When you get a business or real estate loan from a commercial bank, you will usually be required to maintain a *compensating balance* for the loan. Defining this:

A *compensating balance* is the sum of money a commercial bank requires that you keep in your business checking account after making a loan to you. No interest is paid on your compensating balance. And the compensating balance effectively raises your interest cost for your loan.

For example, you borrow $100,000 at 8 percent interest on a discount basis from a commercial bank (identified by the initials N.A. after its name, meaning *National Association*). The bank's compensating balance requirement is 5 percent of the loan, or $5,000. When you borrow on a discount basis, the year's interest is deducted in advance. Your first year's interest on your $100,000 loan is $8,000. Thus, your loan check will be $100,000 less the $5,000 compensating balance, less the $8,000 interest for the first year, for a total of $87,000. Your true interest cost will be 9.2 percent, as opposed to the stated 8 percent.

While this may seem expensive, if you can put your $87,000 to work to earn 5 or 10 times that amount, your compensating balance and interest costs are small compared to your profit. And your interest cost is tax-deductible against your profits.

Some people reverse the compensating bank approach. Let's say you have a multifamily income property that allows you to keep an average business checking account balance of $5,000, as in the preceding example. You are not paid any interest on this account. So:

1. **You go to your friendly banker loan officer** and tell that person that your average business checking account balance is $5,000.
2. **"How much," you ask the loan officer,** "could I borrow using that $5,000 as a compensating balance?"
3. **"Well," the loan officer replies,** "if we lent you $100,000 we'd ask you to keep 5 percent, or $5,000, as your compensating balance. So we'll lend you $100,000 at 8 percent discount interest on your $5,000 compensating balance."
4. **With this in hand,** you apply for a $100,000 loan, if this amount will meet your money needs. You've used a compensating balance as an asset to fund your loan!

Today, some commercial banks shorten the name of this form of asset lending to *balances*. No matter what the name, the same general rules apply. So, if you want a compensating-balance loan, you must:

1. **Have a business checking account** at a commercial bank in which you keep a cash balance of at least $5,000; $25,000 is much better!

2. **Follow the bank's rules.** Try to shortcut the rules and you'll lose your chances of getting the loan you seek.

Some commercial banks require a much larger percentage balance than the 5 percent example given previously. Thus, some banks may require a 10 percent balance; others, 20 percent.

Use a Balloon Loan to Earn More from Your Asset

You can borrow your way to business or real estate riches if your monthly payments on your loan leave enough for you to have a positive cash flow. To reduce your monthly loan payments, use a *balloon loan.*

> A *balloon loan* uses a shorter term (say 10 years) for the full loan repayment with a longer-term (say 30 years) payoff schedule. This reduces your monthly loan payment but requires full repayment at the end of the short term in the form of a lump sum—termed the *balloon.*

The longer, 30-year term is called the *amortization time* and it allows you to get by with a smaller monthly payment while receiving the loan amount you need. For example, let's say you need a $100,000 loan for business or real estate. Here's how it might work out for you:

Loan amount needed	$100,000
Amortization term	30 years
Interest rate for the loan	8 percent
Loan term for balloon	10 years
Monthly payment on 10-year $100,000 loan	$1,210.33
Monthly payment on 30-year $100,000 loan	$733.80
Monthly savings with 10-year balloon loan	$476.53
Annual savings with 10-year balloon loan	$5,518.36

At the end of 10 years you would—of course—owe the balance of the loan amount. At that time you might:

1. **Refinance the loan** with your current lender who knows you and your repayment history. By using your current lender, you won't have to scratch around for a new lender.

2. **Take an equity loan** on the business or real estate to pay off the loan, if the business or real estate is worth more than you paid for it.
3. **Use some of the increased equity** (ownership) you have in the business or real estate asset to take out cash on a tax-free basis to buy another business or more income real estate.

So a balloon loan can be your ticket to riches because it gives you room to maneuver while your business or real estate grows in value. Again, you're using the power of an asset to get the money you need!

Key Ideas for Getting Asset-Based Loans

- **The simplest way** to get asset-based funding for real estate or a business is to use a down payment grant.
- **You can use an option** to control an asset until you sell it at a profit to build your income from the asset. There are several different types of options you can use.
- **Mortgaging out**—that is, getting paid when you take over an income-producing asset—can give you cash in hand at a time when you most need it.
- **You can use debt assumption** for your financing and get an asset for zero cash out of your pocket.
- **Business asset-based loans** can often be obtained quickly.
- **Cash-flow notes** can be a quick and steady source of business financing for you.
- **Paper of various types** can be a sure way for you to get asset-based financing of your business or real estate.
- **SBA loan guarantees** are an excellent source of business funding for you. And today the paperwork is reduced and approvals are faster.
- **Your local state, county, or city government** can be an ideal source of business and real estate money for you.
- **When you're in a hurry** for a business or real estate loan, try the Internet. But be sure to observe the cautions given in this chapter.

(Continued)

- **For a lower-interest-rate business or real estate loan,** apply at a lender that offers LIBOR rates. This can save you lots of money.
- **Put a compensating balance** to work in your business checking account at a commercial bank to give you greater borrowing capacity.
- **Use a balloon loan** to reduce your monthly payments and increase your business or real estate profits.
- **You have a good friend in your author.** You'll find my contact information in the last paragraph of Chapter 8.

CHAPTER

8

Putting It All Together to Get the Money You Need

Y ou now have dozens of ways to get the money you need for your business or real estate funding. In this chapter we bring all these methods together to get you *your* money! And we also give you, my good friend, many additional smart, unique ways for you to get the money you need for your business or real estate deals.

Your main goal—always—is to get you the money you need so you can reach the business or real estate income levels you've set as your target. So let's get you the money—starting right now!

Know the Money Sources You Can Use

When you're looking for money you want to be able to tap into as many sources as possible. Here are 20-plus money sources you should consider using. Most are discussed in detail earlier in this book. Not all the sources listed supply every type of funding you might need. So we've labeled the sources this way:

B—**business loan or funds** of other types (grants, equity capital) for start-up, expansion, machinery, personnel.

RE—**real estate loan or funds** of other types (grants or equity capital) for construction, purchase, rehab, conversion.

P—**personal loan** for debt consolidation, education, vacation, and so on.

Source	Type(s) of Funding
Banks (commercial, savings)	B, RE, P
Mortgage companies	RE
Credit unions (federal, state)	B, RE, P
Angel investors (group, individual)	B, RE
Venture capital	B, RE
Public offerings (Reg A, ULOR)	B, RE
Grants (government, foundations, company)	B, RE, P
Limited partnerships	B, RE
State, county, city agencies	B, RE
Small Business Administration (SBA)	B*, RE**
Private lenders	B, RE
Overseas lenders	B, RE
Small Business Investment Companies (SBIC)	B, RE**
Insurance companies	RE
Factors (for accounts receivable)	B
Commercial finance companies	B
Religious-based groups	B, RE, P
Federal Housing Administration (FHA)	RE*
Veteran's Administration (VA)	B, RE
Export-Import Bank	B
Industrial associations	B
Personal loan companies	P
Small Business Development Companies (SBDC)	B, RE
U.S. Dept. of Agriculture	B, RE
U.S. Dept. of the Interior	B, RE
U.S. Dept. of Education	B
U.S. Dept. of Health and Human Services	B
Relatives, friends	B, RE, P

*Not a direct loan; loan is guaranteed.
**Where real estate is part of the business.

The sources listed here generally make, or guarantee, the types of loans listed. But in some cases, they may make more than the type(s) of loans shown, depending on the situation surrounding a loan. Reg A and ULOR stock offerings as well as grants supply funds in non-loan form. The SBA and FHA guarantee loans. But *all* of these sources can help you get the money you need!

Schedule Your Money-Getting Activities

My Money-Raising Schedule Task	Estimated Time to Complete	Check Off Date Completed
1. Choose type of funding to obtain.	1 week	_____
2. Prepare business plan or grant proposal, depending on type of funding needed.	2 to 3 weeks	_____
3. Have the business plan or grant proposal evaluated.	2 weeks	_____
4. Revise business plan or grant proposal, if necessary.	1 week	_____
5. Contact potential funders; request their application.	2 weeks	_____
6. Prepare working copy of application by copying it for use in a rough draft.	2 days	_____
7. Type loan application or grant proposal.	2 days	_____
8. Submit loan application or grant proposal.	2 days	_____
9. Wait for response from the funders you sent your application to.	2 to 3 weeks	_____
10. Receive funds; or rework the loan or grant application based on advice from the funder.	1 week	_____
11. Resubmit the improved application; wait for response.	2 to 3 weeks	_____
12. Keep trying until you get the funding you seek.	3 to 6 months	_____

Now that your money-getting activities are scheduled, you're ready to get the money you need for your business or real estate moneymaking. Following are a number of proven ways for you bring it all together and get your money. These tips are based on my years of experience lending money to people in many different situations. So read these tips carefully, and use them, my good friend! Remember, you're listening to a lender who wants you to get the money you need. You have an experienced loan officer ready to help you every step of the way!

Don't Be Fooled by Phony Loan Guarantees

Today you'll see many loan offers that seem too good to be true. Thus, you'll see loan deals saying:

- **"Prime Bank Guarantees"** will secure your loan with any lender that wants to work with you.
- **"Prime Bank Letters of Credit"** (LC) will ensure your loan; buy the LC and you'll never have to worry about getting a loan again.
- **"Prime World Bank Debentures"** can get you the big loan you seek. You'll see "millions, billions" tossed about in print and online.
- **"ICC 3034 or an ICC 3039"** can be used with a traditional financial instrument—such as a standby, performance, or a commercial letter of credit—and is allegedly produced by the International Chamber of Commerce.

Many of these claims can be false, not for real! So when you're offered any such promise or scheme, get away from it as fast as you can! It's probably a fraud, and you, as a legitimate businessperson, do not want to be associated with it. Instead:

1. **Deal only with established lenders** who have a record of making the type of loan you're looking for.
2. **Submit a typewritten loan application** (or online application) using the lender's form.
3. **Never pay an advance fee** for a so-called loan guarantee to anyone. While some lenders may request a small application fee of $150 to $250 for a real estate loan, this is not an advance fee. Advance-fee front money for "loan guarantees," "processing fees," "travel," of $1,000 to as high as $100,000 for large loans, may be illegal and should *never* be paid! Keep in mind that many lenders who charge a $150 to $250 application fee return this to you if they make the loan you requested.
4. **Be willing to pay** the modest fee of $50, or less, for a credit report that may be charged by some lenders. Again, this is not front money—instead, it is a fee for services rendered. And many lenders will refund such nominal fees when they make the loan to you!

So how can you get legal and honest loan deals? Here are the steps you can follow to ensure that you're not fooled by phony offers:

1. **Know your lender.** Get full data on the kinds of loans the lender makes, the lender's past history, and fees charged.
2. **Refuse to pay any front money** for loan guarantees. Such charges may be illegal. Further, most front money disappears, never to be seen again!
3. **Deal only with reputable lenders** and loan brokers. Their only charge may be a modest fee that is returned to you by the lender when the loan closes and you get your money!

Get Financing from Lenders That Want You

Lender services vary widely. Some lenders offer services that can help you get your business or real estate loan faster. Thus, you'll find lenders who advertise:

- Brokers welcome.
- Brokers protected.
- Brokers wanted.
- Finders wanted.
- Loan originators wanted.

Such lenders are much easier to work with because they're actively seeking new borrowers to whom they can make loans. Why is this? Because these lenders:

- **Need new borrowers** wanting money for business or real estate so the lender can make loans to increase the lender's interest income. (For instance, in the lending organization of which I'm a director, we're constantly seeking new borrowers because we have so much money available that we privately say to each other "We're so liquid [have so much money to lend] that we slosh!")
- **Have easier requirements** to meet to get a loan approved because they want to make more loans.
- **Will allow you to be** your own loan broker and will protect your commission, reducing your overall loan cost.
- **Can help you earn money** as a loan broker if you bring them new business, including your own loan needs!

So how do you find such lenders? It's easy. Decide to specialize in finding these lenders. You:

1. **Read the *IWS Newsletter*** every month where you may find dozens of such lenders listed.
2. **Check your local newspapers** for lenders advertising offers like these.
3. **Search the Internet** for lenders whose ads resemble these offers.
4. **Contact the lenders** you feel would be interested in your money need.
5. **Question the lender** about their need to make new loans. If the need is intense, as it often will be, ask if you can earn a commission by brokering your own loan application to the lender. Some lenders will pay you a commission; others will agree to make the loan to you without paying a commission. Since your goal is to get your loan, take any money offered to you!
6. **Do what your lender requests.** But *never pay any front money* for your loan. If the lender asks for money up front of any amount, go to another lender for your loan. *Remember:* Hungry lenders make more loans!

For Financing Success, Get a Loan Commitment

A loan commitment is a written promise from a lender to make a loan to you or to your business:

- **Of a stated amount**—for example, $100,000, $1 million, $10 million.
- **At a stated rate of interest**—for example, 6 percent, 8 percent, 10 percent, 12 percent.
- **For a named purpose**—such as business purchase, first mortgage on real estate, second mortgage.
- **By a given date**—October 1, 2___; December 1, 2___.

Your loan commitment is often called a *letter of commitment,* or a *commitment letter,* because your written commitment is sent in the form of a letter. Thus, a typical commitment letter might read:

Commitment Letter Example

Bank of _____

Date_____

Dear Mr./Ms. Borrower:

The Bank of_____ hereby agrees to make a 60-month business loan to you in the amount of $500,000 at a simple interest rate of 8 percent by June 1, _____,
repayable principal and interest monthly in the amount of $10,140.00,
provided you supply the following collateral prior to June 1, _____:
_____.

Very truly yours,

A. J. Smith, Senior Vice President

With a commitment letter you are assured that your loan will be made to you, provided you meet the terms of the letter. Thus, with this example letter, you would have to supply the collateral requested. To get a commitment letter:

1. **Fill out** the lender's loan application fully and neatly.
2. **Provide** data on the collateral your lender requests.
3. **Be specific** about the amount of money you need and the purpose for which you need this money.
4. **Ask your lender** for a commitment letter once the lender agrees to make you your loan.
5. **Comply with** the requirements your lender sets up. But *never pay front money for the loan!*

Get Your Loan Faster with a Courtesy Deposit

A courtesy deposit is money you attract to a bank in the form of a savings account or certificate of deposit (CD) purchase. The courtesy deposit:

- **Is designed to make a bank friendlier** to you so your loan application is approved.
- **Cannot be used** as collateral for your loan.
- **Is not made** in your name—it is in the depositor's name.

- **Must be held** in a government-guaranteed account.
- **The deposit is made by someone** other than yourself. You do *not* make the deposit. You just attract the deposit from someone else to the bank you're trying to get a loan from.

"Do all banks welcome courtesy deposits?" you ask. The answer is: It depends on the bank and how anxious it is to attract deposits. Thus:

- **When deposits in a bank** from regular sources have fallen, a bank looks for a larger inflow of cash to use for making new loans. In this case, courtesy deposits are welcomed by the bank.
- **If a bank has a healthy supply** of deposits coming in, courtesy deposits are not sought.
- **Check with your bank** before seeking a courtesy deposit source because you may find that your bank doesn't need such deposits at this time.

If your bank is looking for courtesy deposits and you're looking for a loan from your bank, you could be in a good position to use such a deposit. Here's how to bring these two needs together:

1. **Find a courtesy deposit company** or individual with funds to deposit in a government-insured account. You'll find some of these companies advertising in the *International Wealth Success* newsletter and in the *Wall Street Journal.*
2. **Contact the courtesy deposit company** or individual by phone, e-mail, or postal mail. Ask how much money they have available for deposit. Also, ask what their fee is for making a courtesy deposit to the bank you designate. The usual fee is 5 percent of the amount deposited, or $5,000 for a $100,000 deposit. You pay this fee after your bank notifies you that the deposit was received in good faith.
3. **Contact your bank loan officer.** Ask that person what the effect of a courtesy deposit would be on your loan application if you were to attract a deposit of, say, $100,000 or $200,000? Would the attitude toward your loan application change? The loan officer will give you an accurate answer. This might be "Yes, it will help!" or "No, it won't make a bit of difference!"

You have your answer. Go for the courtesy deposit. Or forget it! Just be sure you get your answer *before* you pay for the courtesy deposit!

Use Seller Financing If You Can—It Will Help You

Seller financing will help you almost every time you use it! Why? Because with seller financing:

- **The seller of a business or income real estate** provides all or some of the needed down payment money through a loan to you, the buyer. You don't usually have to apply to any other lender!
- **Often giving you 100 percent financing** for the business or real estate you buy, which can provide you with an income for as long as you want it and work at it.
- **Meaning that you probably** won't have to go through a credit check to get the financing you need.
- **Allowing you to overcome** a past history of bankruptcy or other problems of slow pay, no pay, and so on.
- **Transferring much larger assets** to people whose credit might not be the best.

"So how can I get seller financing?" you ask. The answer is easy. Take these quick, simple steps:

1. **Pick the business or real estate** you want to buy to earn money from. Be specific. Thus you might write in your notebook: "Buy an auto rental business," or "Buy a 100-unit apartment house."
2. **Look in** your local newspapers, the *IWS Newsletter*, on the Internet, and in industry magazines and newsletters for a business or for income real estate for which the ad says, "Owner financing available," or "Seller will finance," or "Financing available." These lines tell you that seller financing may be available to you.
3. **Contact the seller immediately!** Such offers go fast. You want to be the first in line to take over the real estate or business.
4. **Be completely businesslike** in your approach to the seller. Tell him/her that: (a) You always wanted the type of business

or real estate being offered for sale; (b) you're willing to work long hours to make the business or real estate more successful than it is now; (c) you always pay your bills on time; (d) you're reliable!

5. **Agree to any reasonable terms** the seller offers you, provided you get owner financing and a positive cash flow from the property or business that's enough for your income needs.

6. **Buy the real estate or business** and go all out to make it a big success. Why? Because the more successful you are, the more you'll put in the bank to build your wealth on owner financing!

Apply Success Formulas to Get Good Financing

When you finance a business or real estate, you must be sure you can repay the loan on time. Many BWBs I meet and talk to have mental formulas they use when they're looking at a possible investment. Here's one BWB's success formula that has made him a multimillionaire. He uses it when analyzing a real estate property or a business he wants to buy. His formula is:

Monday, Tuesday, Wednesday, I Expect Favorable, Happy Results.

"So what does this formula have to do with buying a business or income real estate?" you ask. Here's your answer. When checking a business or a real estate property, this investor does not want to overlook any expense he might have with the income stream he's thinking of buying. So, using his saying, which he calls a formula, he remembers:

Monday = M = mortgage payment(s)

Tuesday = T = taxes on the business or real estate

Wednesday = W = water charges

I = I = insurance cost for the business

Expect = E = electric cost

Favorable = F = fuel costs

Happy = H = help (labor costs)

Results = R = repair costs

Not every property will have all these costs. But keeping them in mind using this, or a similar, formula will help you remember key costs you must pay.

Some BWBs start to panic when they see these costs. Don't let this happen to you! Why? Because with a carefully chosen business or property:

- **Your annual income** from the business or property will cover *all* your expenses—that is, *every* expense just listed.
- **Your annual income** from the business or property will also cover *all* your mortgage payments, so the business or real estate is paying for itself.
- **Your annual income** from the business or property will give you a positive cash flow (PCF) every month of the year, if you work your numbers right. And all or most of this money is legally sheltered from taxes by the depreciation on the business assets or building.

So you see, having a positive, pointed mantra formula can help you make big money in business or real estate, using borrowed money! Just be sure that what you finance will pay for itself, plus give you the income you seek!

Obtain Your Business Money from an SBIC

Do you need money for a business start-up? Or for a large real estate project that is part of a business? If you do, then you should consider applying at a Small Business Investment Company (SBIC) for the money you need.

Small Business Investment Companies are private lenders funded in part by loans guaranteed by the Small Business Administration (SBA). Loans are made for almost every usual business need. And SBICs can also furnish venture capital and angel money for a variety of businesses. The types of businesses funded are:

Agriculture	Diversified
Chemical/biotechnology	Education
Construction	Energy/natural resources
Defense/public safety	Finance/insurance

(Continued)

Healthcare	Restaurants/food service
Information technology	Retail sales
Manufacturing	Telecommunications
Publishing/printing	Transportation
Recreation/athletics	

Investment amounts range from less than $500,000 to over $7 million. Start-up and existing businesses are both welcome by most SBICs. Real estate loans or investments are made when the real estate is part of the business itself. For example, if a manufacturing company needs a factory, the SBIC could include purchase of land and one or more buildings as part of its funding package.

To get SBIC funding for your business take these easy steps, starting right now:

1. **Locate an SBIC near you.** You can use the IWS book *Small Business Investment Company Directory* ($20) to do so. (See Appendix.) Or you can go on the Internet to www.sba.gov and find one there.
2. **Call, fax, or write the SBIC** and ask them for their funding guidelines. This info will be sent to you free of charge. In it you'll find typical funding amounts; types of businesses preferred, if any; geographic areas served, and so on.
3. **Fill out the loan application** and send it in. Be sure to type it!

   With a promising business, you could get money you need!

To Get Your Loan Faster, Listen to the Lender

You know you need a business or real estate loan—that's why you're reading this book, good friend of mine. And you do know *what* amount of money you need, for *how* long, and at *which* interest rate. From this point on, to get your loan, you *must* listen to a lender who tells you:

- **What kinds of loans it makes**—business, real estate, refinance, rehab, buy, build, assumable, and so forth.
- **Which loan-to-value ratio it uses**—65 percent, 75 percent, 90 percent, and so on. This fixes the down payment you need. Thus, a 75 percent loan-to-value-ratio on a $100,000 property means you can get a first mortgage for $75,000 (75 percent of

the appraised value of the property, or $100,000). You'd have to find a down payment loan for $25,000 to buy the property with this LTV ratio.

- **When a seller-take-back is allowed** for the down payment—you can get 100 percent financing with the seller lending you the down payment.
- **Which FICO score is acceptable** to the lender—today 600 and above is often sought by many lenders. Others accept 550.
- **When borrower recourse is needed.** This means you must personally assume liability for repaying your loan—pledging assets you own as collateral for the loan.
- **Whether seasoning (a payment history) is needed** for refinancing your asset (a building, land, business, etc.). When no seasoning is required you move ahead faster.
- **Which loans are assumable.** Having an assumable loan means it's easier for you to buy a property. And it's also easier for you to sell the property at a later date.
- **When a balloon loan is allowed** and what type of amortization (payoff schedule) is allowed. With either arrangement your monthly payments are usually lower.
- **What services are offered to borrowers.** Some lenders offer one-on-one loan officer service to every client with step-by-step guidance from the day your loan package is received until your loan check is handed to you, or the money is wired to your bank. For example, as a loan officer, I talk directly to every borrower and advise them on a successful course of action they can take to get their loan. As lenders we *want* to make more loans to qualified borrowers. That's why we spend time with borrowers, helping them get the loan they seek!

Now, how can you listen to your lender? There are a number of ways, each of which is really easy. These ways are:

1. **Get—in writing—a full description** of the services offered by your lender. There is no charge for this info—a lender sends it to you free by fax, e-mail, or postal mail.
2. **Read *all* the material given to you.** This is how you listen to your lender—you analyze all info given to you because doing so allows you to see inside your lender's activities and what it seeks from a borrower.

3. **Seek in your reading the advantages** *you* **need to get your loan.** Thus, allowing a seller take-back, where the seller lends you the down payment, can be a great advantage to you when you're trying to use 100 percent financing.

Listen to your lender and you can grow rich using borrowed money to get started!

Prosper on Lender Balance-Sheet Needs

As I said earlier, I've been in the lending business for a number of years. And all of us lenders have balance-sheet needs. "What are balance-sheet needs?" you ask. Balance-sheet needs are:

- **Loan activity** a lender needs to show its shareholders.
- **Loan activity** a lender needs to show its regulators.
- **Loan activity** a lender needs to earn a profit.

Why does a lender need to show loan activity? Because:

- **Lenders earn more** from the loans they make than from any other investment they're allowed to make.
- **Lenders please their shareholders** when they make lots of good loans to businesses and individuals.
- **Lenders comply with** the wishes of their regulators (state and/or federal) when they make loans locally and nationally.
- **Lenders show the loans they've made** on their monthly balance sheet. The more loans made, the better for the lender!

So how can you capitalize on a lender's balance-sheet needs? You can take these easy steps in getting loans for yourself, or in acting as a loan broker for one or more clients:

1. **Bring as many loans** for yourself, or for others, as you can to selected lenders.
2. **Be sure, in advance,** that the type of loan you're bringing to a lender is the type of loan the lender makes.
3. **Have the amount of the loan being** requested within the range the lender offers. You'll increase your approval chances enormously!

4. **Know in advance** whether you or a borrower you represent will accept the interest rate the lender charges.
5. **Be ready to accept the lender's terms** if you or your client are offered a loan by the lender. Why spend time, energy, and money applying for a loan if you're going to turn it down?
6. **Prosper in your business by getting the loan** you or your client need, while improving your lender's balance sheet. You've made a *win-win* deal for all!

For Loan Success, Use an 80/20 Product

Talk to a business or mortgage broker, private lender, or real estate developer today and you're almost certain to hear mention of an *80/20 product*. So just what is such a product?

- **It is a real estate** or business loan made up of two parts.
- **Part one is** the long-term portion running 15 to 30 years, or longer, covering 80 percent of the cost of the project.
- **Part two is** a short-term loan for 20 percent of the project cost that runs three to five years at a higher interest rate than part one.
- **The combination gives** you 100 percent financing of the project.

"This sounds great," you say. "What are the negatives of such a product?" There are two negatives, namely:

- **Your positive cash flow (PCF)** is lower during your early years of ownership because you're paying off two loans (the 80 percent and 20 percent). This reduces your monthly PCF.
- **You may have to look** for a while to find such products.

If you're willing to accept these challenges, and I think you should do so to get the money you so ardently need, the 80/20 product can be a lifesaver for you. Why? Because:

- **It can get you into a business or real estate** deal with 100 percent financing. This is a goal many BWBs have.
- **The 20 percent loan**—the hard part—can be based on a home equity loan on a single- or multifamily home project.

- **Or the 20 percent can be based on** the future, higher, value of the business or real estate at the end of the time given to pay off the 20 percent portion of the loan.
- **For a business, the 80 percent** can be based on machinery and equipment; the 20 percent is based on known cash flow from the business operations.

So where can you find such 80/20 products? There are a number of places where the 80/20 product is known, is used, and is popular. These places are:

- **Mortgage brokers** specializing in finding lenders in your area.
- **Private lenders** dealing with real estate and/or business loans.
- **New home builders** offering larger homes at higher prices.

All you have to do, my good friend, is decide what type of loan you need—business or real estate. Then start looking for your 80/20 loan. As a subscriber to our *IWS Newsletter,* we'll be happy to help you.

Get Cash Advance Money for Your Business Needs

If you're in business for yourself now, or you plan to buy a going business that accepts credit card charges, here's a great source of money for you. This powerful source of money for your business is *a cash advance against your future credit card sales.* Here's how it works. Let's say you're processing $10,000 per month in credit card charges. Then:

- **You can borrow** anywhere from $5,000 to $100,000 against your future credit card sales.
- **You must have** been in your retail or restaurant business at least two years to be eligible for these cash advance loans.
- **You must have** at least one year left on your store lease, if you rent the space in which you run your business.
- **You must have** acceptable credit—both for the business and yourself personally.
- **You must be** free of any tax liens, bankruptcies, or court judgments against yourself or the business.
- **You must accept** VISA and MasterCard in your credit card processing activities.

Once you get your cash advance you can use the money for any business purpose—such as to expand your store or other facility, advertise to bring in more business, buy machinery or other needed equipment, and so on.

"So how do I pay off my loan?" you ask. Here's the answer to your question:

- **Your lender receives** a small amount of each future credit card charge, which goes toward paying off your loan.
- **You receive** the bulk of every future charge to continue running your business, as usual.
- **You can get** valuable free advice from your lender to help you run your business more efficiently in the future.

You can be approved for this type of borrowing within 24 to 48 hours after you apply. Your loan money generally arrives in 7 to 21 days after you apply for the funding you need. You can get started with this type of funding by just filling out a simple application that you can e-mail, postal mail, or fax to your lender, saving you lots of time in getting your money.

Now that you know this powerful type of funding exists, you can use it these ways:

1. **As a source** of needed business money for yourself.
2. **As a source** of business money for clients needing funding for their business to expand it in any of several ways.

Use a Revolving Line of Credit for Your Money Needs

You can get a revolving line of credit for your business or real estate deals from lenders if you have a known future need for business or real estate money. And your revolving line of credit can go for more than one year, if you wish. Thus:

- **You can tap into**—that is, draw out money from—your credit line any time you need the funds by writing a check.
- **You need pay only** a small *commitment commission*, usually 0.25 to 0.50 percent ($250 to $500 per $100,000 line) at the time the line of credit is offered to you and every year you have your line of credit thereafter.

- **More and more banks are offering** a revolving line of credit to smaller and smaller firms today.
- **Most revolving lines of credit** do not use collateral. That is, the line of credit is based on your company's credit rating. But if you want to, you can use collateral (real estate, machinery, stocks, bonds, etc.) to secure your line of credit. If you do, then your fees and interest are usually lower.

So how can you best go about getting your revolving line of credit? Here are the steps to take, starting right now, remembering that you *must* be in business to get a line of credit:

1. **Write a brief one-page** description of your company, the work it does, what its annual sales are, and the profits for this year and last year. If your firm is new, state this.
2. **State how much you need** in your revolving line of credit. Use a round number—$100,000, instead of $86,750! Why? Because lenders are accustomed to working with round numbers, instead of offbeat numbers!
3. **Tell the lender the time duration** for your revolving line of credit. The most common time frame is one year. But if you need two years, three years, or more, tell the lender that in your description.
4. **Include, with your description**, a filled-out loan application provided by your lender. Submitting this now will speed the decision and get you your money sooner.
5. **If your credit score (FICO) is under 600**, use one of your partners or corporate officers who has a higher credit score as the applicant for the revolving line of credit. Why? Because you'll have a much better chance of being approved with an applicant who has a higher credit score.
6. **Follow *all* the lender's rules**, once you get your revolving line of credit. Treat your lender well and you'll be treated the same way! Every lender appreciates a considerate borrower!

Another way to get a revolving line of credit is to use any securities (stocks or bonds) you or your company own. You can *margin*—that is, borrow—up to 50 percent of the current market value of these securities. Thus, if you own $100,000 in market-value securities, you can obtain a revolving line of credit for $50,000.

Your stockbroker or your bank, depending on who holds your securities, will give you a checkbook allowing you to write checks for up to $50,000 on this account. The interest rate you pay will be somewhat higher than for traditional business loans. But you *will* get the money you need!

How to Borrow for Business with Bad or No Credit

"What can I do," readers ask," to get started in business on borrowed money when:

- **"I'm just 18 years old** and have no credit history?"
- **"My credit score** is in the low 400s because I've had so many 'slow pays' and a bankruptcy two years ago?"

The answer to both these questions, and variations of them, is:

- **You must bring** one or more partners having good credit into your business, giving them a piece of the action from both the income and ownership of the business.
- **Then you build** up, or rebuild, your credit to the point where you can borrow on your own for your next business or real estate deal.
- **Recognize that** taking a partner is the price a BWB pays for having no credit history or weak credit. And even though you may hate taking a partner in, you will at least be making progress toward your goal of owning your own business or income real estate. Without a partner with good credit, you're stuck and really can't get started taking steps toward your goal.

To find a suitable partner to get the money you need to start or buy your own business or income real estate:

1. **Decide** what business you want to go into. Name the business as accurately as you can. Thus, typical businesses you might name are (a) pre-owned recreational vehicle (RV) dealership; (b) 20-unit rental garden apartment house in _____ City; (c) pasta fast-food franchise with a 100-seat dining facility; (d) import/export business of medical supplies, and so on.

2. **Write** a short business plan (two pages at most) telling yourself and others what your business will be, how much you expect to sell (in dollar terms) each year, what your start-up or purchase costs will be, and how much profit you'll earn each of the first three years.

3. **Figure out** what you'll offer a partner who has good credit to come in with you while you do all the work and the partner collects profit as you repay the loan needed to start or buy the business. A good starting point for rewarding your partner(s) is 10 percent ownership plus 20 percent of annual profits.

4. **Use a written agreement** with your partner(s) covering their participation and what they will be paid. Have the agreement prepared by a competent business attorney. Be sure you and your partner sign and date the agreement before you start or buy your business!

5. **Advertise for partners.** You can run free ads in the *IWS Newsletter*. Ads in the Sunday newspaper business section might bring you the partners you seek for your business or real estate.

6. **Go on to build** or improve your credit while you expand your business. Then buy or start your next business or income real estate on your own! All the profits and ownership will be yours! Could you ask for a better deal?

Use an Interest-Only Mortgage

More real estate buyers are seeking interest-only mortgages for the income properties they want to buy. Why is this? Because with an interest-only mortgage:

- **Your** monthly payments are lower.
- **Your** income is higher for the term of the interest-only payments. And your profit is higher.
- **Your** chances of selling or refinancing the property before having to make principal payments are high.

"So how does the interest-only mortgage work?" you ask. Let's look at an apartment house you buy for $650,000. You work out an interest-only mortgage at 8 percent for 30 years, with the first 15 years being interest-only payments. Thus:

- **Monthly** interest-only payment for the first 15 years: $4,333
- **Monthly** interest/principal payment (P&I) over the next 15 years: $6,214
- **Monthly** payment savings for first 15 years: $1,881
- **Monthly** saving × 12: $22,572/year, or $338,580 in 15 years

You save yourself over $338,000 during the first 15 years you own this property. And if you sell it during that time your profit from the sale will be higher because your cost was lower. Or:

- **You could refinance** the apartment house during the first 15 years you own it to take out tax-free cash.
- **If the building** rose $175,000 in value during this time, **you could take $175,000** or more cash out of the apartment house to use for other investments you might want to make.
- **This money is tax-free** when you receive it, and you still own the building and its income!

So how do you get an interest-only mortgage? Here are easy steps for you to follow to get your interest-only mortgage:

1. **Find a building or property** you want to buy. Lenders are reluctant to talk in general terms; they want a specific property.
2. **Know the full details** of the property—its *price*, its *income*, its *expenses*, and the *down payment* being asked for. Know your numbers and money needs!
3. **Prepare a short** (one- or two-page) business plan for the property showing how its income will allow you to make both the interest-only and the principal and interest (P&I) payments from the income the property generates.
4. **Contact mortgage lenders.** Ask for a combined interest-only and P&I loan for the longest term possible—at least 30 years. And get the longest possible interest-only term—at least 15 years. Hold, sell, or refinance, according to your income needs!

Don't Bash Long Money Searches

Everyone wants quick results today. But sometimes speed in raising money is hard to find. So the person or business seeking a loan or other form of funding finds they're applying to lender after lender, or for other types of funding, with constant turndowns. Can this situation be turned into positive results? Yes, it can be! How? (*Note:* While we talk mostly about loans here, the principles apply to every other type of funding—grants, venture capital, public issues, and so on.)

- **Learn from each turndown** by asking the lender or other money supplier why the application was rejected. Get as many details as you can about the turndown.
- **Ask each lender** what other lender might make the loan if you improve your application. Get names of loan officers they know.
- **Continue to apply** to as many lenders as you can, because the more you apply to, the greater your chances of approval.
- **Become an expert** on the type of loan you're seeking—such as a real estate mortgage on income property, business expansion, and so on.
- **Listen intently to every lender** you meet. These people will often reveal what made them approve a loan. Make that part of yours!
- **Build a list of loan sources** based on what you learn from each lender; aim your future applications at similar lenders everywhere.
- **Talk to other borrowers** to learn what they learned getting their loan in the local area—the who, why, what, where, and when.
- **Apply to hundreds of lenders,** if necessary, to get the loan you seek—because, as people say, there's strength in numbers!
- **Recognize that** even if you spend months on finding a suitable loan, the time is short compared to having to work for, and save, the same amount of money as you get from your loan.
- **Be smart when first talking to a lender.** Ask the loan officer to refrain from checking your credit until after he/she tells you—frankly—what the chances are of your getting the loan you're applying for. Don't have your credit checked if the chances are less than 95 percent!

Your long search for a loan or other type of money can be an interesting and rewarding experience, provided you do not become discouraged and give up. One of our BWBs spent an entire summer looking for a $600,000 loan. He got it after applying to 359 different lenders. The first 358 lenders said no. But number 359 said yes!

Was it worth it? *Yes,* he quickly replies. Would he do it again? *Yes,* he quickly replies, again! So will you, when you get your loan, or other form of funding—no matter how long it takes!

Know the Types of Loans Available to You from Private Lenders

We mentioned private lenders briefly in Chapter 1. Now I'd like to give you more detailed information on the range of loans that private lenders make.

Why? Because private lenders may be more interested in making a loan to you than some traditional loan sources. For example, following are some statements some private lenders make in their informational materials. (*Note:* Not all private lenders offer all these features in their loan programs. So check with each lender individually.) Some private lenders offer:

- **Low** initial monthly payment.
- **Balloon mortgages**—5-year/7-year.
- **First-time** buyer programs.
- **Imperfect** credit program.
- **Hard money,** rehab, and construction loans.
- **Average time** to close is 7 days, or less.
- **Borrower's credit rating** is not a factor in approval process.
- **Purchase, and renovate**, non-owner occupied single-family homes.
- **We do not place much emphasis** on your credit history.
- **Many hard-money loans** can be structured so there are no monthly payments.
- **Private "Fast" money** loan programs available in all 50 states.
- **You can receive funding** in days; we can fund deals on the fly.
- **Interest-only payments** for 1 to 5 years.
- **Exceptionally low** rates for our borrowers.
- **No prepayment penalty** when you borrow from us.
- **We allow lots of junior financing;** maybe even 100% of purchase price.
- **Land loans** on its raw, undeveloped state. Use proceeds for land development.
- **Variety of programs**—easy in/easy out; variable/convertible loan.

- **Construction loan** with takeout—short term followed by long term mortgage.
- **No interest payments** for up to 6 months.
- **Points can be rolled** into loan balance at closing.
- **Up to 70% of ARV** (After Repaired Value); interest only.
- **Lenders for any type** of a "make sense" real estate project.
- **All terms** and conditions are negotiable.
- **We do not charge up-front fees** to our borrowers.
- **100% financing on the purchase** of investment properties with credit scores of 700 and above.
- **100% financing on the purchase** of primary residence or first-time home buyers with credit scores of 590 and above.
- **Sub-prime** and hard money loans available.
- **Foreclosures** and bankruptcy okay for borrowers.
- **Property types:** Apartments, office buildings, land only, marinas, mobile home parks, industrial centers, shopping malls and storage facilities.
- **Transaction types:** Acquisition, debt, and construction.
- **Private money available** for all types of real estate investment.
- **Fast, written commitments** lock in your deals.
- **Real estate transactions** that amount to 100% financing can be accomplished in one of two ways through our services.
- **Our specialty is making mortgage loans** to real estate investors.
- **Hard equity financing** is potentially less expensive.
- **We provide hard-money loans** to purchase and renovate non-owner-occupied single-family homes.
- **We often help facilitate financing** on real estate where banks have failed.
- **We are what is referred to** as an "alternative" financial resource.
- **No appraisals for loans** below $250,000. No up-front application fees.
- **Not FICO-score driven** but common-sense driven.
- **Blanket loans** instead of cash down payments.
- **Loans for self-employed**—no-income-qualification loans.
- **Loan-to-value based on** value, not the sales price.
- **Common-sense underwriting** (lending) with credit problems understood.
- **100% credit** tenant financing.
- **Value-added opportunity financing** for our borrowers.
- **Fast money** for "Opportunity Deals."

- **Private Party Funds** come from investors, IRAs and small pension funds.
- **OK to have** sellers carry back.
- **Bad credit** or foreclosure properties OK.
- **Brokers protected** and included in our Fee Agreement.
- **We provide** stretch senior secured loans.
- **We like** difficult loan situations.
- **Cash out** for any reason.
- **We embrace** the challenge of getting the difficult loan funded.
- **Credit history** is not an issue.
- **Loan Brokers**, looking for a good source of private money? We can help.
- **Our investors make loans** that are "outside the box."
- **No-money-down** loans.
- **We loan money** to real estate investors who buy distressed property, rehab and sell, or refinance a few months later.
- **These loans are used to** purchase property, repair it and also finance the closing costs of the loan.
- **Loans are structured** to create a "no-money-out-of-pocket" real estate acquisition.
- **We offer low-down-payment mortgages;** in some cases up to 100% financing.
- **Offering 100% commercial real estate** development and acquisition loans, and 100% financing for residential construction projects.
- **"Proof of Funds"** letters provided.
- **Properties in pre-foreclosure** can be funded by us.
- **We will fund a property** that has been purchased at an auction and has a clear title.
- **Private money for residential properties** up to 100% LTV (Loan to Value)
- **Our goal is to simplify** the borrowing process.
- **We finance 65%** of the "as repaired value" of the home.
- **All residential and commercial lending,** including conventional, jumbo, and hard money.
- **Programs:** Income producing: Acquisitions, Refinance, Cash-out.
- **Broker Referral Fees:** We offer referral fees to brokers who bring us hard-money leads.
- **Turnaround time:** As quickly as 4 days.
- **100% refinance** with credit score of 620.

- **We also have commercial and hard money loan programs** from $500-K and up.
- **100% financing** for investment properties.

There you have more than 70 statements made by a variety of private lenders I've reviewed and analyzed. These statements should convince you that private lenders can help you acquire the real estate or business you seek.

Remember: These statements are those published by lenders in their informational materials. However, not all these statements apply to every lender; in most cases only one or two of the statements may apply to any one lender. So please do *not* hassle me when you find a lender who acts on just one of these statements! As I said earlier in this book: "Listen to your lender; you'll learn!"

As an aside, our *Private Loan Money and Funding Kit*, listed in the Appendix, contains data on the lenders who make the statements given above.

When Are Grants Better for You than Venture Capital?

Venture capital (VC) is available for a number of businesses that are developing products for large markets. And grants may also be available for the same businesses. So which should you take—venture capital or a grant? To decide, remember:

- **Venture capital** is an investment in a corporation—that is, the purchase of stock in your corporation.
- **With venture capital** you give up a portion of your ownership in your corporation—typically 30 to 50 percent.
- **When a large block** of ownership is given up, 50 percent or more, you're an employee once again, working for the venture capitalist.
- **Grants do not require** that you give up any ownership—you own 100 percent of the business to which the grant is made. But your business usually must be organized as a 501(c) not-for-profit entity.
- **A grant may be distributed** in parts—thus, with a $100,000 grant, you may receive $20,000 at a time. This can be highly motivating to you, making you work more for your success.

- **A small grant** may be followed by a big grant if the work is successful and has been done as promised, on time.
- **Most grants** are given for delivering a needed service to a large group of people—marketing is not covered by the grant. So you must find more money for marketing, if you have to sell your services.
- **Plenty of money** is available for grants but it can be slow in being delivered to you because of required paperwork. But you *never* need repay a grant if you do the work for which the grant was made. And you don't have those pesky monthly payments to make!

So if you don't want to give up ownership of your business, you'll take the grant funding. Or, if you need large amounts of money, say $1 million and up, you'll go for the venture capital. To get either type of funding:

1. **Your business must**—in general—be organized as a corporation.
2. **You must be doing** (a) practical research to get a business grant that can lead to useful products for large entities—such as the Department of Defense, U.S. Department of Health, the Office of Homeland Security, State Education Department, City Health Department, State Electric Power Company, and so on; or (b) if you're helping people live a better life, you must deliver practical help that benefits those needing it.
3. **Research you're doing** for a business grant must be conducted in a formal lab or manufacturing setting. It's almost impossible to get a research grant for a home business because agencies want practical results.
4. **Noncorporate grants** are available for small businesses in the fields of book publishing, theater production, and arts (painting, sculpture, music, poetry, and so on) of various types. These are generally obtained from the National Endowment for the Arts and from similar state or city groups. The work being done can be performed at home. Venture capital is, in general, *not* available for these types of activities because they do not meet the profit goals of VC. Health, job training, schooling, and similar grants are available from a number of federal and state agencies, along with foundations and large corporations.

To get the grant you seek, you must submit a proposal detailing (1) how much money you need; (2) the purposes for which the money will be used; and (3) what benefits the public, the government, or other groups will derive from the work. Submit your proposal to government (state, federal) and private grant givers. Full data on successful grantsmanshp is contained in our two grants kits listed in the Appendix.

Zero-Cash Methods for Building Your Wealth

Zero-cash methods can make you rich even when you have no cash, poor credit, no income history, and have difficulty raising money for your business or real estate deals. Why is this? Because:

- **More people** have *no cash* to invest than those who do have cash to invest.
- **Using borrowed money** is a wise way to live your business life because your own money is *not* at risk.
- **Your percent return** is much higher when you use borrowed money to finance your wealth building.

"So how can I get started on zero cash?" you ask. Here are your answers:

1. **Decide** what type of property or business you want to invest in. Is it income real estate? Is it a business? Whatever it is, you *must* know. Once you know, it's easy to start!
2. **Find the property** or business you want to buy or start. Do this by looking in local newspaper real estate or business sections showing properties/businesses for sale.
3. **Contact ads** that interest you. Get full data on price, income, expenses and down payment.
4. **Analyze the data** you receive. You *must* have a positive cash flow (PCF) from your real estate or your business. *Never buy income real estate or a business that does not give you a PFC!*
5. **Make an offer** for the real estate or business based on how much you can earn from the project—after paying *all expenses*, including your long-term mortgage loan *and* your down payment loan or loans.

6. **Complete the deal** and start earning money from your own business! You'll be happier, and richer, than ever.

So what are your keys to zero cash? There are three keys to your getting real estate or a business on zero cash. These keys are:

1. **Your long-term loan** is easy to get because it's based on the value of the property or business. This value is your asset. So look for real estate or a business having a high value for a low price. The value will make your long-term loan easy to get and to repay fully, and on time, even with poor credit.

2. **Your down payment loan** is your key to zero-cash success. So you must be creative about getting it. And you *must* be *realistic* about your down payment loan. Lenders expect to be repaid in *full.*

3. **Your down payment loan** can usually be in the range of $5,000 to $50,000, if you use traditional sources. These sources are: (a) credit card lines of credit; (b) personal loans; (c) seller take-back, called a purchase money (PM) mortgage; (d) loans from relatives or friends; (e) equity loan on your own, a relative's, a friend's, or a partner's property. At the start, don't go for a down payment loan of $500,000 or more! You won't get it. Go for $10,000 to $50,000 and you'll probably get it!

How to Do a Business Plan Quickly, without Pain

In almost every chapter in this book we've recommended that you prepare a business plan to help get the funding you need. The simple truth, my good friend, is this: To get a loan quickly today you should have a business plan.

Why? For a number of good reasons. A business plan:

1. **Shows your lender, or other funder,** you are serious about your business goals and that you've thought out how you'll reach them while repaying your loan fully and on time.

2. **Helps you** see ahead to your future steps in business and how you'll take each step to reach your financial goals.

3. **Lets you concentrate** on building your business to its maximum income without having to worry about money.

"So," you ask, "how do I do a business plan quickly, without pain?" Here's your answer—quickly and easily:

1. **Find a business plan** for your type of business that you like and which says what you want to say about your business, in a way that you believe is accurate and that you admire.
2. **Substitute** your company's name for the firm name in the business plan. Then pattern the description of your company on the business plan you like. You put your own words in for what you believe your company can and will do in your business as time goes on. *Do not copy the sample business plan!* Just use it as a guide in preparing your own business plan.
3. **Do the same** for the other sections of your business plan for the information on competition, the market, your management team, your marketing plans, and financial projections. Be sure to put your own numbers and words in your business plan!
4. **Again,** *do not* **copy the other business plan!** Just use the business plan as a *guide* to your own plan. With the other plan as a guide you can concentrate on what you will do with your company, its sales, and its people.
5. **Use a business plan** for both business and real estate projects. Why? Because lenders admire business and real estate operators who take the time to prepare a sound business plan for their projects. Very few business and real estate entrepreneurs do business plans voluntarily. Most have to be asked to prepare their business plan. Approach your money sources with a business plan in hand and your chances of a *yes* answer are much stronger! For example, I recently advised a yacht club on getting a $1.6 million loan from the lender for whom I'm a director. The commodore followed my suggestions on doing a business plan and we were happy to make the loan at a lower-than-usual interest rate. The business plan was the clincher in the loan approval. We wired the money to the club's bank account. This borrower listened to me, as a lender, as I advised you earlier in this chapter. And he got the loan, which was his goal! And that's my goal for you, my good friend.

Never complain about having to do a business plan! Why? Because a business plan can get *you* the real estate or business loan you seek faster than you ever thought possible! Do a good business plan and you can get almost every loan you ever apply for! Just be sure *not to copy* another company's business plan! Instead, use it as a *guide* to doing yours so you get the funding you need for your real estate or business!

As an aside, when I'm talking as a loan officer to a potential borrower about his/her business plan, we often get into the details of the business. Such a conversation can go on for 30 minutes, or longer. As the conversation develops I can feel a warmth and genuine friendship grow between the borrower and myself. Result? The loan is usually *approved*!

As a final proof to you of the effectiveness of a business plan, I offer this letter that came by e-mail as I was finishing this chapter:

> I read your book *How to Make Millions in Real Estate in Three Years Starting with No Cash*. From there I built a business plan which I followed. From December 30 last year to June 21 this year, I purchased $900,000 worth of property.
>
> **(By e-mail from South Dakota)**

This reader acquired $150,000 per month of real estate, for a total of $900,000 in just six months! Why? Because he had a business plan! So you see the power you can command when you do your business plan. Please listen to me, my good friend! And hear me. I have only *your* success to sell you!

Key to Putting It All together to Get Your Money

- Know the money sources **you can use.**
- Schedule **your money-getting activities.**
- Don't be fooled **by phony loan guarantees.**
- Get financing **from lenders that want you.**
- For financing success **get a loan commitment from your lender.**

(Continued)

- Use a courtesy deposit **to get easier access to loans.**
- Try to get seller financing—**it can really help you.**
- Apply success formulas **to get good financing.**
- Don't overlook **getting your financing from an SBIC.**
- To get your loan faster, **listen to your lender.**
- Prosper on lender **balance-sheet needs.**
- For borrowing success, **focus on an 80/20 product.**
- Get a cash advance **for your business money needs.**
- Use a revolving line of credit **for quick access to money.**
- You *can* borrow for your business—**even with no, or bad, credit.**
- Use an interest-only mortgage **for high profits and earnings.**
- Recognize that a long search for money **may be the best learning experience for yourself and your real estate or business activities.**
- Private lenders may be your best source **of loans because they offer so many different types.**
- There are times when a grant **may be better than venture capital for you.**
- Use zero-cash methods **to build your real estate and business wealth.**
- Do your business plan **quickly, and without pain. It can get you your loan, grant, or venture capital!**

To Reach the Author

Several times in this book you've read that I'm your friend and that you can reach me in various ways. Thus, you can call me at 516-766-5850 from 8 A.M. to 10 P.M. Eastern time. Or you can fax me at 516-766-5919, 24/7. You can e-mail me at tyghicks@aol.com, 24/7. My web site is www.iwsmoney.com, and www.iws-inc.com. And I have several blogs that you can find on www.blogspot.com. I'll answer your questions and give you advice. You must remember, however, that I give first attention to my newsletter subscribers. Why? Because they deserve it. You can reach me by postal mail at my business, IWS, Inc., P.O. Box 186, Merrick, NY 11566-0186.

Appendix

USEFUL FINANCING AND REAL ESTATE BOOKS, REPORTS, TRAINING COURSES, AND NEWSLETTERS FOR BEGINNING AND EXPERIENCED WEALTH BUILDERS

You *can* build your business and real estate riches on borrowed money faster! How? By getting more know-how about financing methods and sources of money for your business and real estate investments. As has often been said, knowledge is power! And Ralph Waldo Emerson said, "Only an inventor knows how to borrow, and every man is or should be an inventor!"

Here are a number of sources of financing information and data for your business and real estate needs that you'll find helpful, and profitable.

Real Estate Self-Study Success Kits, Books, Reports, and Newsletters

The following success kits, books, reports, and newsletters are available from the publishing company of which your author, Tyler G. Hicks, is president. You can obtain any of these publications by (1) sending a check or money order by postal mail to the address listed here, (2) calling by telephone to order by credit card, (3) faxing your credit card order, or (4) ordering on the Internet.

To order by mail, send a check or money order for the amount listed to IWS, Inc., P.O. Box 186, Merrick, NY 11566-0186.

To order by credit card, call 516-766-5850, day or night. Have your credit card ready when you call. To fax your credit card order, send the name(s) of the product(s) you want, and their prices, along with your credit card number, its expiration date, three-digit security code, and your telephone number via fax to 516-766-5919, 24/7.

To order on the Internet, go to the web site www.iwsmoney .com or www.iws-inc.com, and use the shopping cart for your order, after finding the product(s) you want. Or you can use your PayPal account to order on the Internet.

Now here's a listing of kits, books, and newsletters that we offer that can be helpful to you in your financing activities for business or real estate.

Success Kits

Success Kits are self-study, hands-on, practical courses to train yourself for a new or expanded business. These kits emphasize quick learning to help you earn money as soon as you can. Many kit courses are written by your author, Tyler G. Hicks.

Private Money Loan and Funding Kit by Tyler G. Hicks gives methods you can use to borrow money for business or real estate from private lenders of many different types. This kit supplies you with more than 100 private lenders—name, address, telephone/fax, e-mail—plus data on the types of loans each lender makes; typical amounts; any geographic preferences; and their approach to lending vis-à-vis credit scores, past payment history, and so on. This list is the only such compilation the publisher is aware of and it could be your source of private money for your business or real estate investments. Other information given in the kit includes successful loan packaging techniques, plus numerous ways to get 100 percent financing of your transactions. $100. Over 400 pages, 8.5 × 11 inches, paperback.

Venture Capital Funding Kit by Tyler G. Hicks shows you how to raise venture capital for yourself or others. This kit gives ways that you can use to get started in just hours raising the venture money you or a client may need for business or real estate transactions. You see how to prepare your executive summary to get the attention of a venture capitalist. And you're shown how to have others prepare a comprehensive business plan to present to a venture capitalist. The kit includes examples of successful business plans you can use as a guide. Venture capital is not a loan; hence, there are no monthly repayments to make. $100. 300 pages, 8.5 × 11 inches, paperback.

Loans by Phone Kit shows you how and where to get real estate, business, and personal loans by telephone. With just 32 words and 15 seconds of time you can determine if a lender is interested in the loan you seek for yourself, or for someone who is your client if you're working as a loan broker or a finder. This kit gives you hundreds of telephone lenders. About half have toll-free 800 or similar numbers, meaning that your call is free of long-distance charges. Typical agreement forms are also included in the kit. Written by Tyler G. Hicks. $100. Over 150 pages, 8.5 × 11 inches, paperback.

Small Business Loan Kit covers acting as an agent for a factoring lender to get loans for either yourself or clients who have done work for large organizations such as a city, state, university, hospital, large corporation, and so on. You earn a commission when you bring loan clients to the factoring lender and the loan is made. As a purchaser-user of this kit you are provided with two lenders with whom the publisher of the kit has a referral relationship. You can call these factors (one on the East Coast and one on the West Coast) and they'll set you up immediately when you tell them you're using this kit. $100. Over 300 pages, 8.5 × 11 inches, paperback.

Fast Financing of Your Real Estate Fortune Success Kit shows you how to raise money for real estate deals. You can move ahead faster if you can finance your real estate quickly and easily. This kit concentrates on getting the money you need for your real estate deals. The kit gives you more than 2,000 lenders of real estate money all over the United States. It includes private lenders who may consider your real estate deal. And the kit shows you how and where to find deals that return a big income to you but are easier to finance than you might think. $99.50. Seven speed-read books, 523 pages, 8.5 × 11 inches, paperback.

Financial Broker/Finder/Business Broker/Business Consultant Kit shows you how to start your own private business as a financial broker, finder, business broker, or consultant. As a financial broker you find business or real estate money for yourself, for companies, or for individuals, and you are paid a fee after the loan is obtained by you or your client. As a finder you are paid a fee for finding things (real estate, money, raw materials, etc.) for firms or people. As a business broker you help in the buying or selling of a business—again for a fee. This big kit shows you how to collect fees for the work you do for your clients. The kit also contains typical agreements used in the business, tells you what fees to charge, gives you a prewritten news release to get free publicity for your business, and includes four colorful membership certificates (each 8 × 10 inches). $99.50. 12 speed-read books, 500 pages, 8.5 × 11 inches; four membership certificates.

Mega-Money Methods Kit covers the raising of large amounts of money (multimillions) for real estate and business projects of all types. Some of these projects may be offshore in overseas countries. The kit shows you how to prepare loan packages for very large loans, where to get financing for such loans, what fees to charge when the loan is obtained, plus much more. Using this kit, the BWB should be able to prepare effective loan requests for large amounts of money for viable projects. The kit also gives a list of international offshore lenders for big real estate and business projects. Written by Tyler G. Hicks. $100. Over 200 pages, 8.5 × 11 inches, paperback.

Single-Family Home Riches Kit by Tyler G. Hicks covers earning money from single-family homes (SFH) by owning them and renting them out, flipping them, leasing them to Section 8 tenants, and so on. Topics include: 10 ways to get your SFH on zero cash using other people's money (OPM); where to find big cash-flow properties; how to buy low and sell high today; when—and where—to get zero-down finance; getting hard-money loans today; investing with little risk to your money; easy ways to make big flipping profits; fast financing methods for real estate start-up; and getting started with poor, or no, credit. Includes four big bonuses—*Home Buying Guide, Getting the Best Mortgage, Handbook of Adjustable-Rate Mortgages,* and the Ty Hicks *Fast Financing Methods for Real Estate Start-up and Expansion.* $150. 500 pages, 8.5 × 11 inches, paperback.

Multifamily Home and Small Office Building Riches Kit shows beginning and experienced real estate wealth builders how to acquire multifamily properties (apartment houses, garden- and townhouse multifamily units, and small office buildings) and operate them profitably. This big kit shows where to get the money to buy multifamily properties, what to do to get started on zero cash, when is the best time to start building your real estate fortune in multifamily units, which multifamily units can build your real estate fortune the fastest. Covers loans, grants, lines of credit, and other smart ways to finance these cash "cows." Details seller financing, equity loans, Section 8 bonuses, and more than 3,000 lenders for multifamily properties. Includes four valuable bonuses on private lenders, real estate foreclosure documents, free weekly sales data, and lenders for large multifamily projects. Written by Tyler G. Hicks and other authors. $150. 504 pages, 8.5 × 11 inches, paperback.

Foreclosures and Other Distressed Properties Kit shows you—with six audiocassette tapes (or four CDs) and a comprehensive manual—how and where to find, and buy, foreclosed and other distressed properties of all types. The kit gives names, addresses, and other data about agencies offering foreclosed properties—often at bargain prices. It also presents forms giving examples of actual foreclosure documents and paperwork, and shows how to evaluate properties you're considering buying. $53.95. More than 150 pages, 8.5 × 11 inches, paperback; six cassette audiotapes, or four CDs—please specify which you prefer.

How to Build Your Real Estate Fortune Today in a Real Estate Investment Trust Kit shows you how to start a REIT to finance any type of real estate in which you want to invest to earn money. The kit gives you the exact steps to take to raise money from either private or public sources. Today's REITs raise millions for almost every type of real estate used by human beings—multifamily residential (apartment houses), factories, marinas, hotels, motels, shopping malls, nursing homes, hospitals, and so on. Real estate investment trusts can own these types of properties, lend on them (issue mortgages), or make a combination of these investments.

Written by Tyler G. Hicks. $100. Over 150 pages, 8.5 × 11 inches, paperback.

Low-Cost Real Estate Loan Getters Kit shows the user how to get real estate loans either for a client or for themselves. The kit lists hundreds of active real estate lenders seeking to make first and/or junior mortgage loans for a variety of property types. Loan amounts range from a few thousand dollars to many millions, depending on the property, its location, and its value. The kit presents typical application and agreement forms for use in securing real estate loans. No license is required to obtain loans for oneself using the data in this kit. This big kit provides step-by-step guidance for obtaining the real estate loan(s) of the user's choice. Written by Tyler G. Hicks. $100. Over 150 pages, 8.5 × 11 inches, paperback.

Grants and Fund Raising Success Kit by Tyler G. Hicks shows you how to get business or real estate grants for yourself or your firm. The kit gives you typical money grant offers you can use to obtain funds. You're shown what a foundation looks for when you submit a grant proposal. And, especially important, the kit shows you how to use your grant money profitably. You also learn what makes a good grant proposal. You're provided with sources of hundreds of grant-making organizations and a directory of federal government grant programs. $99.50. 500 pages, 8.5 × 11 inches, paperback.

Phone-In Mail-In Grants Kit written by Tyler G. Hicks gives you a quick way to find out whether a grant you're seeking is of any interest to a grantor—an organization that makes grants for worthy causes. Each year more than $30 billion in grants is paid out to not-for-profit groups, companies, and individuals for thousands of different projects. This big kit helps you get some of this money for yourself or your organization. The kit shows you each step to take to get your grant. And you're given a method to narrow down your prospects so you get your grant quickly. $100. Over 300 pages, 8.5 × 11 inches, paperback.

Real Estate Riches Success Kit shows you how to make big money in real estate as an income property owner, a mortgage broker, mortgage banker, real estate investment trust operator, mortgage money broker, raw land investor, and industrial property owner. This is a general kit covering many key aspects of real estate ownership, financing, and investment. It includes numerous financing sources for your real estate wealth building. The kit also covers how to buy real estate for the lowest price (down payments of no cash can sometimes be arranged) and how to run your real estate for the biggest profits. Written by Tyler G. Hicks. $99.50. Six speed-read books, 446 pages, 8.5 × 11 inches, paperback.

Zero-Cash Success Techniques Kit shows you how to get started in income real estate or in your own business venture with no cash of your own. This big kit includes a special book by Ty Hicks titled *Zero Cash Takeovers of Real Estate and Business*, plus a 58-minute audiocassette tape by him titled *Small Business Financing*. In the tape Ty talks to you, telling you how you can get started in income real estate or in your own business without cash and with few credit checks. $99.50. Seven speed-read books, 876 pages, 8.5 × 11 inches, paperback; 58-minute audiocassette tape or CD.

Business Plan Kit shows you how to prepare a business plan both for a business and for a real estate investment transaction. This big kit guides you step-by-step to exactly what to include in your business plan. Two actual examples of successful business plans are given—one for a business corporation and the other for a real estate investment. Since almost every business and income real estate loan requires a business plan, this kit should be part of your business library. $39.50. 200 pages, 8.5 × 11 inches, paperback.

Commercial Real Estate Riches Kit shows you how to build your fortune in commercial real estate investing in office buildings, hotels, motels, shopping malls, marinas, tennis courts, golf courses, and so on. This big kit gives you step-by-step ways to find, evaluate, finance, and buy such properties that will give you a positive cash flow. The kit includes 3,000 lenders you can work with. Written by Tyler G. Hicks, this big kit can get you started building your fortune in commercial real estate. $150. 400 pages, 8.5 × 11 inches, paperback.

ULOR U-7 Finance Kit gives you the steps you can follow to use the Uniform Limited Offering Registration to raise up to $1 million a year for your business or real estate investments by selling stock in your corporation to the public or to private investors.

Using this way of raising money either privately or publicly, you can get up to $1 million per year in no-repay financing you need for a business or for income real estate. $100. 200 pages, 8 × 11 inches, paperback.

Real Estate Books

Limited Partnership Agreement with Questions and Answers gives an example of a typical real estate limited partnership agreement prepared by a legal team, along with focused questions and answers about limited partnerships and how you can use them to finance your business or real estate transactions. This is an excellent introduction to this important way of raising money for your business. $30. 100 pages, 8.5 × 11 inches, paperback.

Comprehensive Loan Sources for Business and Real Estate gives hundreds of lenders' names, addresses, telephone numbers, and types of loans made. $25. 136 pages, 8.5 × 11 inches, paperback.

Directory of 2,500 Active Real Estate Lenders lists 2,500 names, addresses, and telephone numbers of direct lenders or sources of information on possible lenders for real estate of many types. It also lists lenders nationwide for a variety of real estate projects—from single-family homes to multi-unit residential buildings. $25. 197 pages, 8.5 × 11 inches, paperback.

Diversified Loan Sources for Business and Real Estate gives hundreds of lenders' names, addresses, telephone numbers, and lending guidelines for business and real estate loans of many different types. $25. 136 pages, 8.5 × 11 inches, paperback.

Selected Lenders for Commercial and Residential Construction Loans gives more than 150 lenders making building and/or renovation loans for almost every type of structure known. This is the only source of such lenders that the publisher is aware of today. Lenders listed make loans principally in the United States; some of the lenders listed also make loans in Canada and internationally. The lenders listed offer innovative financing to fit nearly every construction job met. With this book you can easily survey, compare, and contact more than 150 construction lenders and financing programs. $29.50. 100 pages, 8.5 × 11 inches, paperback.

Sources of Canadian Financing for Real Estate and Business lists more than 1,000 selected financing and loan sources in Canada. This is the only such source of financing information that the publisher is aware of today. The book gives descriptions of the largest lenders and loan programs. Loans included are commercial and residential first and second mortgages, mortgage refinancing and renewal, personal loans, business operating and working capital loans, and loans for professionals such as medical doctors, dentists, lawyers, architects, and so on. Data includes loan amounts, loan program options, and typical sample loan applications. $29.50. 100 pages, 8.5 × 11 inches, paperback.

Financing for Religious Organizations and Places of Worship. Financing for religious organizations is a large and growing market. Banks and commercial finance companies provide more than $800 million in bond financing to these organizations every year. Loans are available for land purchase, construction, renovation of existing structures, expansion of athletic fields, parking lots, social buildings, and so on. This book gives some 100 sources of the special type of funding religious organizations need. Included is a description of each lender, the type of funding it provides, application data, and so on. $29.50. 100 pages, 8.5 × 11 inches, paperback.

Directory of 600+ Personal Loan Lenders lists more than 600 personal loan lenders with their names, addresses, telephone numbers, and fax numbers. Using this book you can apply for the personal loan you need, either locally or at a distance. $25. 48 pages, 8.5 × 11 inches, paperback.

Directory of 500+ Internet Lenders lists Internet lenders for personal/general loans, residential and commercial mortgage loans, subprime loans, construction loans, private-money and hard-money loans, venture capital, small business investment companies, private financing, commercial loans, no-income-verification loans, and international Internet loan sources

(Canada, France, Germany, India, Japan, Switzerland, United Kingdom). $50. 50 pages, 8.5 × 11 inches, paperback.

How Anyone Can Prosper and Get Wealthy Trading Country Land, by Frank Moss, shows how to acquire wealth and have fun trading in country land. Covers supply and demand, starting your own home-based spare-time moneymaking business buying and selling woodlands, estimating value, time/distance analysis, plus much more. Using this book, a person can get started in this lucrative part of today's real estate market. $21.50. More than 100 pages, 8.5 × 11 inches, paperback.

How to Be a Second Mortgage Loan Broker, by Richard Brisky, gives complete details on how to set up your office, find clients, locate lenders, and negotiate with clients and lenders; what fees to charge; how to comply with any licensing laws in your area of business; what files to keep; plus much more. Using this book, a person can get started in this lucrative aspect of today's real estate market. $25. 100 pages, 8.5 × 11 inches, paperback.

How to Create Your Own Real Estate Fortune, by Jens Nielsen, covers investment opportunities in real estate, leveraging, depreciation, tax rules, remodeling your purchases, buy-and-leaseback, understanding your financing, plus much more. $17.50. 117 pages, 8.5 × 11 inches, paperback.

Rapid Real Estate and Business Loan-Getting Methods, by Tyler G. Hicks, gives innovative techniques to get loans; ways in which real estate can make you rich, getting free of the 9-to-5 grind; new steps to getting venture capital; smart-money ways to get loans; plus many other ideas for real estate and business financing. $25.00. 96 pages, 8.5 × 11 inches, paperback.

How to Make Your Fortune in Real Estate Second Mortgages, by Tyler G. Hicks, covers second mortgages, how a second mortgage finder works, registering your firm, running ads, finding capital, expanding the business, limited partnerships, plus much more. $17.50. 100 pages, 8.5 × 11 inches, paperback.

How to Borrow Your Way to Real Estate Riches Using Government Sources, compiled by Tyler G. Hicks, lists numerous mortgage loans and guarantees, loan purposes, amounts, terms, financing charges, types of structures financed, loan-to-value ratio, special factors, plus much more. $17.50. 88 pages, 8.5 × 11 inches, paperback.

Business Capital Sources lists more than 1,500 lenders for business and real estate, including banks, insurance companies, commercial finance firms, venture capitalists, and so on. $20. 150 pages, 8.5 × 11 inches, paperback.

Small Business Investment Company Directory lists several hundred SBICs with full data on the types of investments they make in small businesses and needed real estate. The book also gives tips on wise financial management for small businesses. $20. 135 pages, 8.5 × 11 inches, paperback.

Wall Street Syndicators and New Offering Briefs gives actual examples of numerous small-company offerings in going public. It describes the business, number of shares offered, type of management, and so on. $20. 35 pages, 8.5 × 11 inches, paperback.

How to Acquire $1 Million in Income Real Estate in One Year Using Borrowed Money in Your Free Time by Tyler G. Hicks. This valuable guide shows you how to borrow the money needed to invest in income-producing real estate to build your wealth. Topics include choosing the type of property to invest in; 49 types of mortgages you can use; getting financing even with poor credit; using property appreciation to build your wealth; getting loans on the Internet; dealing with private lenders; and much more. $14.95. 268 pages, 5⅜ × 8 inches, paperback.

209 Fast Spare-Time Ways to Build Zero Cash Into 7 Figures a Year in Real Estate by Tyler G. Hicks. This valuable guide helps both new and experienced real estate investors build wealth in properties of all types. The book focuses on using borrowed money to start and expand your real estate business. Many letters from beginning wealth builders show how they're using the principles given in the book to build their real estate fortune. The book covers every type of income property you might wish to own and earn money from. $14.95. 272 pages, 5⅜ × 8 inches, paperback.

How to Make Millions in Real Estate in 3 Years Starting with No Cash by Tyler G. Hicks covers: why real estate is financially valuable to you, how to finance your real estate fortune, your keys to 5,000 sources of real estate finance, how to avoid beginners' mistakes in real estate, seven lucky steps to becoming a real estate millionaire, take the raw land route to wealth, make residential properties your wealth source, commercial and industrial property, how to leverage properties, unusual real estate wealth techniques, limited partnerships in real estate, go the condo route. $25.00. 282 pages 5⅜ × 8 inches, paperback.

Real Estate Reports

The following eight real estate reports cover various aspects of property financing. Each report is 8.5 × 11 inches in size and presents essential information on getting money for the real estate transaction detailed in the report. Most are based on actual transactions that took place.

Neighborhood and Convenience Shopping Center Loan Package, Report, M-1. Example of a typical successful loan package. $12.50, 40 pages.

Downtown Office Building Loan Package, M-2. Example of a successful loan package for an office building. $12.50, 24 pages.

Single-Family Home Foreclosure Business Plan, M-3. Shows how money could be raised to buy single-family home foreclosures and rent them out or resell them for a profit. $12.50, 24 pages.

Single-Family Home Income Property Business Plan, M-4. Shows how money could be made by owning a string of single-family homes that you rent to tenants for a profit. $12.50, 24 pages.

High-Rise Apartment-Building Loan Package and Business Plan, M-5. Presents a comprehensive loan package and business plan for the financing and operation of a multifamily apartment building. $12.50, 24 pages.

Refinancing Proposal for a Multifamily Apartment House, M-6. Shows how a large apartment house can be refinanced to enhance its competitive position in its marketplace. $12.50, 61 pages.

FHA Multifamily Building Loan Package and Business Plan, M-7. Shows a typical loan package and business plan that complies with FHA requirements. $12.50, 24 pages.

Offering Circular for a Real Estate Mortgage Company, M-8. Real-life example of an actual offering circular used to raise money for an actual mortgage company formed by a BWB. $12.50, 50 pages.

Newsletters

International Wealth Success, Ty Hicks' monthly newsletter. This 16-page newsletter covers loan and grant sources, real estate opportunities, business opportunities, import-export, mail order, and a variety of other topics on earning money in your own business. Every one-year or longer subscriber can run one, or more, free classified ads of 60 (or fewer) words, or several one-inch display ads, free of charge, in the newsletter each month. Ads can be for money wanted, business opportunities, or money available. The newsletter has worldwide circulation, giving readers and advertisers extremely broad coverage. Started in January 1967, the newsletter has been published continuously every month since that date. $24.00 per year. 16 pages per issue plus additional inserts, 8.5 × 11 inches.

Money Watch Bulletin gives a monthly coverage of more than 100 active lenders for real estate, business, and personal use. The newsletter gives each lender's name, address, and telephone number. In some cases the lender's funding guidelines are also given, along with other helpful information about the lender. All lender names were obtained during the preceding two weeks; the data is therefore right up-to-date. In addition, lenders' names are supplied on self-stick labels on an occasional basis. The bulletin also covers venture capital, accounts receivable financing, government mortgage guarantees, overseas lenders, and Canadian lenders. Institutions listed include banks, mortgage brokers, credit unions, private lenders, and so on. Subscribers can run free classified ads monthly in the bulletin. $95.00 per year. 12 issues, 20 pages each, 8.5 × 11 inches.

Books on Financing Techniques for Business and Real Estate from John Wiley & Sons

The following books are available from John Wiley & Sons, Inc., 111 River St., Hoboken, NJ 07030, telephone 201-748-6000. Books listed here range from beginners' guides to helpful dictionaries and comprehensive references. Call the company to learn how you can order their books, or visit their web site, www.wiley.com.

Business Finance

Bradley, W. J., William Benjamin, Joel B. Margulis, and Gerald A. Benjamin, *Angel Capital* (2002), paperback, $19.95.

Butler, Kirt, *Multinational Finance* (2008), $69.95.

Cardis, Joel, Sam Kirschner, Stan Richelson, Jason Kirschner, and Hildy Richelson, *Venture Capital: The Definitive Guide for Entrepreneurs, Investors, and Practitioners* (2001), $43.00.

Cartwright, Roger, *Going Global* (2002), paperback, $19.95.

Faguet, Dmitri, *Practical Financial Management* (2003), cloth, $75.00.

Fight, Andrew, *E-Finance* (2002), paperback, $19.95.

Goldstein, Arnold, *How to Buy a Great Business with No Cash Down* (1991), paperback, $31.95.

Hill, Brian, and Dee Power, *Inside Secrets to Venture Capital* (2001), paperback, $49.95.

Kotler, Philip, Hermawan Kartajaya, and S. David Young, *Attracting Investors: A Marketing Approach to Finding Funds for Your Business* (2004), paperback, $29.95.

McGarty, Terrence P., *Business Plans That Win Venture Capital* (1989), paperback, $352.00.

Preston, Susan L., *Angel Financing for Entrepreneurs: Early-Stage Funding for Long-Term Success* (2007), $39.95.

Stern, Joel M., and Donald Chew Jr., *The Revolution in Corporate Finance* (2003), paperback, $77.95.

Real Estate

Achenbach, George, *Goldmining in Foreclosure Properties* (2003), paperback, $27.95.

Albrecht, Donna G., *Buying a Home When You're Single* (2001), paperback, $14.95.

Arnold, Alvin L., *The Arnold Encyclopedia of Real Estate* (1993), paperback, $426.00.

Berges, Steve, *The Complete Guide to Buying and Selling Apartment Buildings* (2004), paperback, $26.95.

Berges, Steve, *The Complete Guide to Flipping Properties* (2003), paperback, $19.95.

Boiron, Pierre, *Commercial Real Estate Investing in Canada* (2008), $200.00.

Boroson, Warren, and Ken Austin, *The Home Buyer's Inspection Guide* (1993), paperback, $19.95.

Carey, Chantal, and Bill Carey, *The New Path to Real Estate Wealth: Earning Without Owning*, paperback, $19.95.

Cummings, Jack, *The Tax-Free Exchange Loophole: How Real Estate Investors Can Profit from the 1031 Exchange* (2005), $34.95.

DeRoos, Dolf, and Gene Burns, *The Insider's Guide to 52 Homes in 52 Weeks: Acquire Your Real Estate Fortune Today* (2006), $16.95.

Edmunds, Gillette, and James Keene, *Retire on the House: Using Real Estate to Secure Your Retirement* (2005), $18.95.

Eldred, Gary W., *The Complete Guide to Second Homes for Vacations, Retirement, and Investment* (1999), paperback, $19.95.

Eldred, Gary W., *The 106 Common Mistakes Homebuyers Make (and How to Avoid Them)* (2005), paperback, $16.05.

Eldred, Gary W., *Trump University Real Estate 101: Building Wealth with Real Estate Investments* (2006), $21.95.

Finkel, David, *The Real Estate Fast Track: How to Create $5,000 to $50,000 Per Month Real Estate Cash Flow* (2006), $19.95.

Irwin, Robert and Ganz, David L., *The 90 Second Lawyer Guide to Buying Real Estate* (1997), paperback, $19.95.

Larsen, James E., *Core Concepts of Real Estate Principles and Practices* (2003), paperback, $51.95.

Lucier, Thomas, *How to Make Money with Real Estate Options: Low-Cost, Low-Risk, High-Profit Strategies for Controlling Undervalued Property . . . Without the Burdens of Ownership* (2005), paperback, $24.95.

Lumley, James E. A., *Challenge Your Taxes: Homeowners Guide to Reducing Property Taxes* (1998), paperback, $19.95.

Lumley, James, E. A., *5 Magic Paths to Making a Fortune in Real Estate* (2004), paperback, $16.95.

Masters, Nicholas, *How to Make Money in Commercial Real Estate: For the Small Investor* (2006), $40.00.

Molloy, William J., *The Complete Home Buyer's Bible* (1996), hardcover, $29.95.

Shemin, Robert, *Unlimited Riches: Making Your Fortune in Real Estate Investing* (2003), e-book, $24.95.

Shim, Jae K., Joel G. Siegel, and Stephen W. Hartman, *Dictionary of Real Estate* (1995), paperback, $24.95.

About the Author

Tyler G. Hicks is an experienced financial and business adviser and investor. He is also director of a large lending organization that has made millions of dollars of business, personal, and real estate loans throughout the United States, and overseas. During his career he has served as a loan officer for this same lending organization, approving thousands of loan applications. Later, he was elected President and Chairman of the Board of Directors. He is also the author of a number of best-selling books on business, real estate, and engineering. His most recent business book is *How to Acquire $1 Million in Income Real Estate in One Year Using Borrowed Money in Your Free Time* (John Wiley & Sons, 2006). He is also president of International Wealth Success, Inc., and editor of their two newsletters dealing with small business finance.

Index